THE MONKEY
AND THE MONEY

Bezahlmöglichkeiten
Kasse 1
geschlossen
VISA
Bankomat
Mark Pig. Sp. Kellner
20 00

Dr KJELL A. NORDSTRÖM

THE MONKEY AND THE MONEY

A history of capitalism

TRANSLATED BY : RUTH URBOM
EDITED BY : JAN RYDÉN BONMOT

BOKFÖRLAGET STOLPE

A FEW WORDS AT THE START   7

1   **A MIRACLE**   In which an ape discovers the magic of trade and is transformed into an accountant.   9

2   **MONEY AND BANKING**   In which the ape invents money and banking, and we find out how the gold standard became the debt standard.   21

3   **A GLOBAL BRING-YOUR-OWN PARTY**   In which the ape closes some gates and opens others, then starts exchanging things with the whole world.   43

4   **A MAGICAL MECHANISM**   In which we meet the moral philosopher Adam Smith and see our ape transformed into Scrooge McDuck – and learn why the invisible hand needs rules in order to work properly.   59

5   **CAPITAL**   In which we examine what capital is, find out how technology can involve cooperation and take part in the launch of a stock market.   75

6   **THE EARTH AND GROWTH**   In which we build megacities, let our cows graze outdoors, and enjoy coffee, cake and doughnuts.   91

7   **A LITTLE HAPPINESS**   In which we consider why wealthy people are often portrayed as evil, and whether more money really makes you happier – and if so, how much money is best?   109

8   **CURIOUSER AND CURIOUSER**   In which the ape and capital head out into cyberspace, fall down a rabbit hole, colonise the future and trade in derivatives and bitcoin.   133

9   **UPROAR IN THE GLOBAL VILLAGE**   In which the ape manages to open and close a fast-food restaurant, and the Empire strikes back.   155

10   **WHAT HAS THE APE LEARNED?**   In which we fast-forward through history and economics – and possibly end up with some new insights.   173

WANT TO FIND OUT MORE?   190

There's something I want.

Just like any other person who undertakes something – building a house, writing a song or starting a family – there's something I want.

Or, if you want to be picky, there are two things I want.

The first thing I want is to try, once and for all, to explain that companies, money and other things related to the world of economics are not expressions of some sort of evil. Economics is simply our attempt to make life as good as possible in a world of limited resources. It's about budgeting. All the shopping malls, all the banks, all the massive quantities of goods and services we're surrounded by – ultimately, they're all expressions of our desire for happiness. As we will see in this book, way back at the dawn of time we discovered a principle so powerful that it would eventually make the entire world into a single vast marketplace. We discovered the principle of exchange. And there's really nothing strange about it. After all, everyone wants to maximise their happiness. If you want to be critical, you could say that, over time, we have developed an addiction. You could say our pursuit of happiness has gone into overdrive and now threatens to destroy us and our planet. That's a matter I will leave for you, the reader, to decide.

The second thing I want is simply to make economics a bit more fun and accessible. Many people find money, business and other aspects of economics not just incomprehensible but downright boring. As I hope this book will show, most things in the world of economics are entirely comprehensible. And when things are comprehensible, they're usually a little more fun.

A number of extraordinarily generous, talented people have helped to ensure that *The Monkey and the Money* did not remain a mere idea in my head.

Jan Rydén Bonmot shared his wisdom, his patience and his playful intellect to help me see beyond my own horizon. Thank you, Jan, for all our amazing discussions, laughs and excellent glasses of wine. You are a true scholar.

And thank you to Patrik Instedt. You are a magnificent wizard and artist. Your illustrations are not merely gorgeous and brilliant; they are true art, with all that that entails, spurring observers to insight and contemplation.

With my publishing team at Bokförlaget Stolpe, led by Marika Stolpe, guiding the way to the finished book with equal measures of firmness, love and thoughtfulness, things could only go well.

Last but certainly not least, I would like to send my huge thanks and love to Karin af Klintberg, the demon producer.

If I am the father of *The Monkey and the Money*, then you are its mother.

STOCKHOLM, SEPTEMBER 2022

Dr Kjell A. Nordström

A MIRACLE

In which an ape
discovers the magic
of trade and is
transformed into
an accountant.

WANDEL
DURCH
HANDEL
Friends
Forever

APES THAT EXCHANGE THINGS.
That is what we are. It was true in the distant past, and it's still true now.

A roaming, near-hairless ape that wants to survive and shag.

Nothing out of the ordinary, so to speak. Same as any other animal, and for our closest living relatives – chimpanzees, bonobos, gorillas and orangutans – life is mainly about themselves. For a long time, we tried to see ourselves as unique. Different from animals. Today, though, we recognise the folly of that view. We are descended from apes. That's just how it is.

We evolved in Africa some two to three million years ago. Over the years, our desire to survive has taken us to every corner of the globe. We ventured out into the world and eventually adapted to every possible climate and circumstance. We left behind the vast majority of our large family of animals as we went out to conquer the world. Looking back, it seems highly improbable that we – apes underdressed for the occasion, feeling the cold – should have gone on to construct a 5,500-mile-long brick wall along a mountain range in northern China, take photos on the surface of the Moon and, on top of everything else, muddle up our planet's entire climate.

We've been on a long journey – in every way, not just in terms of time. On our way out of Africa and up to the present day, we've done more than merely discover new places and adapt to them. Our brains have also changed over time. We're not entirely certain why, but most scientists now agree that our intellectual functions such as thinking, emotions, memory and more – collectively called cognitive functions – have developed along the way. At some point between 70,000 and 30,000 years ago, our brains started to function differently. For some reason, we got smarter. Our upgraded cognitive functions set the stage for many of the crucial steps we would later take. But our story begins long before we became so clever.

Quite early on in our two-million-year journey to the present, an ape discovered that it could trade one thing for another. The ape also learned that trading things could make shagging and life in general easier. Presumably, the apes didn't think much more about it back then. But, for a little while, life undoubtedly felt a bit better. A tiny seed was planted. Perhaps it was possible to trade other things too.

Let's try to look at what *really* happened. At first, it didn't seem like much to get excited about. A few figs and some nuts changed hands. In terms of geography, they moved a short distance, from one ape to another. Nothing remarkable. The fruit and nuts remained the same, physically. The apes were the same as before. Nothing was added. Nothing was taken away. The only thing that happened was that some small edible items were moved from one context – one ape – to another. But that is precisely where something happened that would later affect our entire planet. That *something* is the smallest constituent element of every business transaction.

The *something* that happened was that *both* apes were suddenly better off than before.

They both felt they were in a slightly better position than before the exchange.

Having *both* nuts *and* figs was better than just having one or the other.

And, as if that weren't enough, *neither of the apes was worse off.*

It's almost too good to be true.

A miracle.

Of course, our apes and their thoughts and feelings are made up. We actually know next to nothing about early humans' day-to-day lives. There are great gaps in our knowledge. There are no written records to consult, and scholars disagree about many things. As a result, the theories and ideas advanced by academics come under intense scrutiny. We lived in small groups that hunted and gathered foodstuffs to survive – that much we do know. And, for this story, that's enough to serve as a starting point: prehistoric humans lived in small nomadic groups, and hunted, gathered and made the things they needed to survive. That was the scale of our lives for hundreds of thousands of years. In fact, people lived in those conditions for so long that many evolutionary psychologists today say that the reason we feel pressured and stressed lies in the clash between the modern world and that hunter-gatherer mentality. Human psychology and biology are still key economic drivers. We are evolving very slowly on that level. We still want to eat tasty things, have fun and live in comfort.

Our little story also brings us to another important line of thought. In that first exchange, the most important thing was not the items that were traded but the happiness that arose from the transaction. That is the purpose of the economy. If we can imagine a means of somehow measuring happiness or joy, it's entirely reasonable to believe that both apes were happier after the nut–fig exchange than before. You don't need archaeology, evolutionary psychology or any other branch of science to deduce that figs *and* nuts, rather than *just* figs or *just* nuts, are what most people prefer. So it seems as though some sort of happiness or joy is generated in the exchange of one thing for another. If you wanted to be a bit more dramatic, you could say that *something is created from nothing –* something that feels better and more valuable to those involved. Perhaps there is something else we ought to observe before we leave the savannah and travel forward through time. Primatologists say that no other species of ape besides us trades things with one other. It is obviously difficult to get anything from a chimpanzee or gorilla in an exchange. They don't exchange things voluntarily. They might steal things from one another within their troop. Maybe they give each other things? But this mutual exchanging of things seems to be unique to us. It's one of the behaviours that make us human.

The path by which we went from being hunter-gatherers in southern Africa to something resembling our current lifestyle is largely obscured in the mists of time. But we do know a few things. Other theories are the result of guesses based on studies of small clay shards and, more recently, DNA analyses. We know that it started with a great migration. At some point, we trekked out of Africa – north towards Egypt, then east and west to populate the world. But we were still hunters and gatherers. We still lived in caves and painted graffiti on walls. Some people crafted funny little sculptures. As we spread across the globe, travelling on foot, we almost certainly exchanged a few things from time to time. But our lives still centred around hunting, gathering and migrating. Artistically inclined individuals left behind small objects here and there. Hundreds of millennia passed.

But then, one day, someone had an idea. We started to plant crops. Instead of moving on when the berries and deer grew scarce, we stayed in the same place. We no longer gobbled up everything growing in one area before heading off. We started to tame both animals and nature.

Then, some 5,000 years ago, between the great Euphrates and Tigris rivers in present-day Iraq, the world's first civilisation arose in Mesopotamia. Agriculture gave rise to more developments. Above all, it meant the end of nomadic life for most of us. We established permanent settlements, and it is no exaggeration to say that a new era dawned. We invented the plough. We built irrigation channels. Invented the wheel. Began writing. Began to calculate. Accumulated stores of grain. Built cities.

Cities and trade go together. There were plenty of people to trade with in Mesopotamia's bustling cities. The first cities were meeting places for people eager to trade. In fact, trading is the reason cities exist. The primary characteristic of a city is that it contains many people in a small area. Most of them are keen on trading and exchanging. That's why they're there. Now, the trading moved up a gear. It became so advanced, so all-encompassing, we could no longer keep track of who traded what with whom. That set the stage for another innovation that would shape us and accompany us: we created the first written languages. They were used for – you guessed it – trade and bookkeeping. To keep track of all the exchanges between various parties and who owed what, we started to inscribe little figures on clay tablets. We drew an ox's head and decided that an amphora symbolised wine. But there were a lot of oxen and amphorae, and the clay dried out quickly. So the drawings became more simplified, in a system called cuneiform.

Funnily enough, the first person mentioned by name in writing was a bookkeeper called Kushim. He lived in the city of Uruk and signed a clay tablet for a consignment of grain: '29,086 measures of barley, 37 months. Kushim.' Something had really happened here. Our nomadic ape had lost most of his hair and become a well-organised, clothes-wearing urban resident. He – if we can assume Kushim was a he – also seemed to like beer. Eighteen of Kushim's clay tablets have been preserved. Some of them record amounts received, or what we now call debits, on one side. The reverse side shows what we modern urbanites call credits: things that are supplied. There are clay tablets with malt and hops on one side, and the other side shows – you guessed it – beer. So our bookkeeper Kushim was a city dweller who drank beer. An early hipster. His job mainly involved clay tablets. Not too onerous; it was quite a good life. Things were going well. The ape had come quite a long way.

The idea of moving to the city in Mesopotamia several thousand years ago was the same as it is for people today who leave the countryside and move to cities like Lagos, Istanbul, Vancouver or Shenzhen. You can become something other than what your parents were. In short, it represents the hope of a better life. There are plenty of other people in the city, so you can specialise in something you're particularly good at. Something that's difficult or impossible to do in a village or rural area with just a few residents, where most people end up doing a little of everything.

If you migrated to a city like Uruk, you might become a manual labourer, digging irrigation channels, building city walls, roads or houses; or you might become a servant, waiting on city residents who are already successful and well established. Maybe you could do some sort of handiwork, like brewing beer or making amphorae? As a craftsperson, you might be able to sell things and earn more than you would have made staying in the village where you were born. Perhaps you could weave cloth? Or you could become a merchant, a specialist in exchanges, making deals day in, day out. If you were unfortunate enough to be a slave, you could actually buy your own freedom if you saved up enough money – right there and then, according to Babylonian law.

Early cities probably resembled cities today, a hotchpotch of people and markets, sometimes confusing and chaotic. But, if we looked behind the jumble of people, animals and smells in an early city, we would find – in a slightly refined form – countless instances, both small and large, of trading and exchange. And every exchange of goods or services generated *value*. Both parties emerged slightly better off. No wonder cities have stuck around and got larger. Ultimately, they become a sort of pulsating organism that generates hope and success.

Now that we know a bit about trading and we have an inkling of what a market can do for us as people, perhaps this would be a good place to take a moment to consider what a market is *not*. A marketplace is *not* like a pizza: a fixed amount of something that can be shared but can never grow. If you get half a pizza from me, then I only have half left. If you get the whole pizza, I have nothing and you have everything. It's easy to think that's how it works. There's only one pizza, and we have to fight over it. If one of us gets more, the other gets less. And vice versa. In other words, a zero-sum game. But that's not how a marketplace works.

The miracle is that *both* parties can end up better off. An exchange can turn out particularly well if you find the perfect person to exchange with. It should be someone who places a high value on your skills or the thing you have, who also happens to possess something you want at that time. In cities or at a marketplace, there are a great many people with whom to trade. There's a reason we use the term *market* economy. The market or bazaar is the magical place where it all happens, where there is hope of improving one's position. The bigger the market, the greater the hope. Over time, the surrounding city becomes a little, or rather a larger, extension of the marketplace.

The chance of finding a match increases dramatically in the city, compared with standing on a dusty rural road, hoping the right person will come along, or sitting in a forest clearing, trying to sell the bread you've baked. So far, we've only been talking about a barter economy in a city. When we add money, or silver, as a payment method to this market square, the chances of making favourable transactions increases many times over.

In Mesopotamia, people started using pieces of silver wire as a standardised means of payment, carrying it in a spool and snipping off a length when it was time to pay. That's it, the transaction is done. Much easier than leading an ox to the market to exchange it for a basket of fresh fish and a couple of barrels of beer. Especially if the beer is only worth a quarter of an ox and the fish is barely worth an ox tongue. By using the silver wire, and with all the people on every street corner in the market-place, new opportunities for exchanges arose all the time. More and more people were better off. Prosperity increased, and things continued in the same way for a long time – for several millennia in Mesopotamia, in fact.

So markets and marketplaces are not a zero-sum game. If that were the case, we would have lost interest in them long ago. Instead, both parties come out ahead. The pizza gets bigger, so to speak – sometimes doubling or more in size. There really is no set limit on how big it can get. There can be pizza for everyone. All you can eat! Unlimited buffet! That's not to say that both parties earn the same on a transaction. In the best cases, the profit is shared equally, but just as often one party benefits a little more. Or a lot more. Perhaps because they know something the other party doesn't know. Perhaps they start out with more assets and can negotiate harder, with no fear of missing out on the deal. Exchanges and deals are not fair at the individual level. Not everyone is happy on every occasion, but the vast majority are a little better off. That's why cities, exchanges and marketplaces have hung in there and flourished over the millennia, in spite of overcrowding, dirt and epidemics. Large numbers of people in a small space have always presented what a modern urban planner would call a challenge.

There is another aspect of economics – namely, commerce and prosperity – that we will encounter again and again throughout world history. Surpluses transformed our way of living. With large numbers of people in one place, they began to exchange ideas as well as goods. The world's first civilisations arose in cities like Uruk, Nineveh, Ur and Babylon, with art, architecture, taxation, mathematics, laws, astronomy and poetry. Now that people no longer had to spend all day gathering food, they had the time and resources for other things. Cuneiform writing, which started as a way of recording transactions involving grain, has also preserved the *Epic of Gilgamesh* for us. This epic poem recounts the legend of King Gilgamesh of Uruk, a superhero and demigod, and serves as a model for so many tales and legends to come later. A little idea, almost self-evident, about exchanging things had come into its own. And it was only a hint of what was in store.

The history of Mesopotamia and its sophisticated cities can also give us some indications of what the market is not good at. This category includes things that cannot be acquired by trading: things that are free. Air is one example. Or seawater. It's obvious, in a way. They are ubiquitous and do not need to be transported to a market. The problem, though, is that, if something is free, we overexploit it. We take as much of it as we can. If it's free to pollute, we pollute. For example, nobody owns the air. It has no price. And, if something has no price, it doesn't exist. Not in Uruk and not in New York. That's how we lived, up until a few decades ago.

Only when a British economist by the name of Nicholas Stern put a price on changes in the climate did global decision-makers start to take notice. When *The Stern Review* was published in 2006, it spurred intense debate about threats to our environment and the climate. Stern calculated that it was far cheaper to stop climate change now than to let it continue. The consequences of global warming would entail costs of at least 5%, and perhaps as much as 20%, of global GDP. That's the total of everything produced in the world in one year. Stopping global warming would cost 1%, and 1% is less than 20%. That made us wake up. The climate and the environment were clearly not free.

We could make a very long list of all the ways in which we have overexploited the natural world. Mesopotamia, Babylonia and Assyria had agriculture that depended on artificial irrigation, with ingenious channels criss-crossing the landscape. The land blossomed. If you have visited Iraq recently or seen news coverage on TV, you know that the area does not look like that any longer. With every passing year, the water evaporated, leaving behind traces of salt. The next year, another tiny amount of salt. And the next year. Over time, the soil was depleted. That wasn't free, either. The plough, perhaps invented by an acquaintance of Kushim the bookkeeper, might have been part of the problem as well. Ploughing increases yields from the earth in the short term, but reduces them in the long term. Every year, a millimetre-thick layer of soil loses its microorganisms, its biological vitality. If you continue ploughing for 500 to 1,000 years, you will use up between half a metre and one metre of topsoil. That's how deep the layer of soil is that provides us with food. Many agriculture-based civilisations averaged a lifespan of between 500 and 1,000 years. We still use many of those practices today. We seem to have a little difficulty with that stuff about short-term and long-term impacts. Especially when the things we're exploiting don't have a price tag.

Back to city life. Today, we often talk about the market. We use that term to refer to more than just two apes innocently exchanging nuts and figs. We use it to mean a group or crowd of people. Sometimes all people. The analogy evokes a romantic image of trading in a market square, vendors offering their wares for sale, tables groaning with goods in marvellous colours. Hustle and bustle, a clamour of voices. Buyers strolling among the market stalls, feeling the goods, sampling their smells, haggling, bargaining.

The first bazaars were established 3,000 years ago, in the Middle East. That's where Kushim lived. The word *bazaar* comes from Persian. Merchants' stalls would line a narrow lane covered by an arched roof. Often there would be a whole district of covered streets, arch after arch, in the semi-darkness, bustling with merchants, financiers and the craftspeople who produced and sold goods. The word market has a wider context, referring to bustling city life, exchanges between people, the lively city square and the bazaar with all its smells on the one hand, but it can also be something impersonal. It can be something beyond us.

Many of us might have some scenes from the Hollywood movie *Wall Street* stored in our memory. Stock-market trading. Men in white shirts, shouting, rushing around, waving pieces of paper. Slips of paper fluttering in the air. A bell ringing. The market goes up, the market goes down. The market crashes. The market recovers. 'The market reacts positively to the central bank's decision.' But what is it really, this market? And how does it work? Is it evil?

This book will attempt to answer these questions. It is primarily about exchanges – transactions – at the dawn of time, as well as here and now in our ultra-modern society. Our focus is not on *what* we exchange, but on the *fact* that we exchange things, and the meaning this has acquired. The narrative begins several million years ago with a couple of fictional apes who exchanged things with one another and became happier as a result.

They discovered a principle so powerful and beneficial that it eventually came to dominate our lives and therefore our history.

As we shall see, much later in this story, the principle envelops the entire world in a dense fog of transactions, where everyone participates, exchanging everything. That fog eventually gets a name, gains a fraternity of experts and its own branch of science: economics.

Many people would say that that innocent exchange of items long ago later got out of hand and went too far. And they're probably right. The Earth's climate and ecosystem have been affected – by us.

Our activity – or more accurately, our hyperactivity – has created the environmental crisis. The Industrial Revolution, which completely reshaped our lives over the past two centuries, would have been unthinkable without a complex web of exchanges. But, as everyone knows, revolutions have never been a walk in the park. Perhaps that happiness mechanism we discovered at the dawn of time cannot continue for ever. There is something tempting and addictive about everything that produces happiness. Insatiable, we want more. And more. Never before have we conducted as many transactions as we do now. Everyone is trading with everyone else, all day, all night, all year – a machine that never stands still. Just look at a shopping centre anywhere in the world on an ordinary Saturday. These are vast decorated temples, built for sheer orgies of transactions. Places where we go shopping have themselves become tourist destinations.

This is a book about our tremendous zeal for exchanging things.

About happiness.

About why money exists.

And, above all, about how the world came to be conquered by one little idea: capitalism.

MONEY AND BANKING

In which the ape invents
money and banking,
and we find out how
the gold standard became
the debt standard.

CASH. MOOLAH. READIES. BACON. DOUGH.
Few things have as many nicknames as money.

Suddenly, one day, it was just there and entered our lives.

Some people say it's taken over our lives.

But where did it come from, originally?

And what *is* money, actually?

Like everything else that doesn't exist in nature, money comes from our playful, inventive brains. That's where it all happens. Exchanging things with others turned out to be a small innovation with major benefits. The most obvious benefit was that we no longer needed to do everything ourselves. Life is a little better when we can help one another. Ultimately, bartering is a form of cooperation that can involve a large number of individuals.

Not everyone needs to go out fishing and gathering nuts. If you happen to find enough nuts, you can always exchange some for fish or something else you need. That's good – and practical. You can also specialise and become really good at something. One or more people in the group might become superstars at fishing in the creek; others might figure out where to find the biggest, best berries. And we can probably sort out who does what, when everyone no longer does everything.

As we shall see later on, this is one of the linchpins of a smoothly functioning group. Each member contributes what they do best. And best of all, this practice is good for the group, society and the individual.

Even so, bartering has clear downsides as well. There are major practical considerations. There are good reasons why we moved on from a simple barter economy in its original form. It's awkward and impractical to drag fish, nuts, eggs and other items around. Fish soon rots, and eggs break easily. Nowadays, we would call these logistics and warehousing issues. Fresh produce is particularly tricky in that regard. Perishability makes it hard to save anything for the future. Even if you landed a bumper catch of fish or managed to drive a whole herd of deer into a trap, you would have problems storing any of it.

It's easier with things that don't have a best-before date.

Maybe prehistoric people exchanged services as well. When we do things for each other, there are no storage problems. It's perfectly reasonable to think that idea occurred just as early on as trading goods, or even earlier. A back scratch is exchanged for a thorough scalp grooming. Exchanging services is practical and contributes to improved well-being and cohesion in the group.

The biggest drawback of bartering is that you and the other person each have to have something the other one wants, otherwise there will be no exchange. No deal. The whole transaction process can easily come to a halt.

But all these practical problems have a solution. In fact, they are quite easy to fix – in our minds, at any rate. In fairy tales, anything is possible. It ought to be possible to come up with an item that is free from any of the disadvantages that make bartering so difficult. What we need to invent is an item that is easy to carry around, that has no annoying best-before date and weighs little or nothing. It should also be completely standardised and easy to store. It must not rot, decay or otherwise go bad. And, last but not least, this *invented* item also needs to be *magically* appealing. The sort of thing everybody wants. Always. If we had that sort of imaginary item, people could exchange every other item for it. Everybody wants it. All the time.

In an exercise almost like playing make-believe or a board game, a group of people can agree to create a pretend item that is so appealing, they can then exchange it for anything else. In fact, that's exactly what we did. We made up – yes, actually made up – items that have no function other than to be exchangeable for other items. They cannot be used for anything else. Sure, it sounds strange, but let's let our imagination roam a bit more. In order to make these made-up items exist in the real world and not just our imagination, we endeavoured to make them visible and tangible. We have used all sorts of things, including stones, shells, metals and other materials that are relatively standardised, easy to carry and able to be stored. Now our made-up idea has almost become reality. *Money.*

We can trace the notion of this made-up item far back in history. Moreover, it seems to have arisen independently in several places around the world, as is often the case with good ideas. That's not surprising. The problems of the barter economy were presumably similar everywhere. The Chinese started using snail shells 3,500 years ago, and various forms of silver started to be used as payment in Mesopotamia around the same time. In the previous chapter, we saw how Kushim the beer-drinking bookkeeper and his contemporaries took a spool of silver wire to the market. When it was time to pay, they would snip off an appropriate-length piece. Quick and convenient, it was an early version of present-day electronic payments.

Various metals – most often gold, silver or bronze – were found to be suitable materials to use in manufacturing this made-up item. Clearly, metals do not rot. They are relatively easy to carry around and generally durable – almost matching our imaginary ideal. For a long time, our made-up item consisted of various naturally occurring objects or metals. In the next stage, it started to resemble something we can recognise from our own era.

Coins were first used in Lydia, a small city-state in present-day Turkey, in the seventh century BCE. The king of Lydia came up with the idea of putting his official stamp on each coin to guarantee its precise weight and quality, and this idea was a success. The more standardised the made-up item became, the better it worked. The king's stamped coins were made from a material called electrum, an alloy of silver and gold. Each coin had to weigh exactly the same as 168 grains of wheat. People often attempted to tamper with the metal content. Stamped coins helped merchants save time and hassle, because they no longer had to weigh and examine each coin. Have you ever tried weighing 168 grains of wheat? Exactly. So it's easy to see why stamped, standardised coins were an improvement. Coins needed to be simple to use.

The first paper banknotes appeared much later, in the tenth century AD, in China. This represented a further step: value had now become entirely symbolic. There was no more metal, not even a few wheat grains in weight. People making transactions had to put their trust in a piece of paper, believing it to be desirable and to have value. As we have seen, everything depends on people wanting that piece of paper; that's when this business with made-up items functions properly. As we shall see later on, sometimes things went well, other times not so well. If a society is fairly stable, with clear laws, rules and enforcement, it can work; you can rely on the issuers and trust that forgers will get caught.

The first European banknotes arrived half a millennium later – and Sweden is where it happened. We can gain insights into the origins of Sweden's paper money and its banking system by tracing the route of an explorer. An enterprising gentleman by the name of Johan Palmstruch (1611–71) paved the way in Stockholm, in 1661. As Sweden's first bank director, he owned his own bank – called Stockholms Banco – and began issuing banknotes.

Palmstruch was a very cosmopolitan fellow. He was born in Riga, which was part of Poland at the time. The city was conquered by Sweden and became part of the Swedish Empire when he was around ten years of age. A decade or so later, he fled to Amsterdam, where he married a Dutch woman. In those days, Amsterdam was the place to be – it was the Silicon Valley or Uruk of its time. The economy was booming, fuelled by the Dutch East India Company. Amsterdam also offered great individual freedom, religious freedom and freedom of the press, attracting philosophers and artists. People could think freely and develop new ideas. The painter Rembrandt moved there. The philosopher Spinoza lived there. Many books were published. The philosopher René Descartes also lived there, in exile from France, before moving to Stockholm (as Palmstruch also did), where he caught a cold and died. Palmstruch worked as a merchant in Amsterdam, but he also spent some time in prison. His search for new opportunities apparently led him in various directions. From Amsterdam, he took the concept of banking to Stockholm. He planned to open a bank that would accept deposits and lend money – the traditional role of a bank. But Palmstruch would add his own personal touch with an innovation.

Palmstruch pitched his banking concept to the king of Sweden, who was not entirely convinced. It took Palmstruch three attempts to persuade the king to allow him to set up a bank. Consent was granted on condition that he paid half the profits into the state's coffers. Palmstruch's innovation – or his unique selling point, as we might say today – was that, instead of lending copper coins, his bank would issue notes with fixed denominations written on them. A sort of promissory note. In simple terms, such a note is an agreement stating that the bearer has a deposit at the bank. The notes issued by Palmstruch's bank carried a statement, written in archaic Swedish, reading, 'The Bearer of this Credit Paper is entitled to demand 100 Dalers in Silver Coins at Stockholms Banco.' It was a contract, in other words. Each contract, or credit note, was individually numbered and bore eight signatures, ten stamps and a seal. Everything was done by the book, all to generate assurances and trust. Receipts for loans, where people filled in specific amounts, had been around for a long time. The innovation here was that the notes were in fixed denominations *and* that they were not linked to a particular transaction.

Palmstruch's credit notes quickly became popular – hugely popular. They were far more practical than the heavy copper and silver coins, some of which were so heavy that people had to transport them in a cart. They were also standardised, like the aforementioned king of Lydia's coins. Unfortunately, though, Stockholms Banco issued more notes than they could redeem. Public trust in the bank took a hit, and the value of the notes started to decline. The Swedish state stepped in and banned the credit notes. A few years later, the first bank in Europe to issue banknotes went bust. Palmstruch, its founder, was sentenced to death.

Sweden's parliament, the Riksdag, bought up what was left of Stockholms Banco and – hey presto – transformed it into a nationalised bank, called Riksens Ständers Bank. Today it is known as the Riksbank, the world's oldest central bank. The adventurer, prison inmate and financial innovator Johan Palmstruch was ultimately pardoned, but died soon after his release. Although Stockholms Banco was no more, the idea of paper banknotes remained. In the mid to late 19th century, more private commercial banks started to spring up in Sweden – and in the rest of the Western world. They also issued their own banknotes. Amazingly, up until 1904, there were between ten and fifteen banks issuing their own banknotes in Sweden alone. That was the year the Riksbank took over. Today, having a single issuer seems obvious, but it was not at the time.

In any event, the central bank had to make a case for its monopoly on issuing banknotes. Their reasoning went like this: if there are multiple banks printing money, the state cannot increase the money supply through the Riksbank at times when the economy needs a boost – or, on the contrary, reduce the money supply when the economy overheats. Creating your own money also happens to be *highly profitable*. The Riksbank and the Swedish state wanted to have that revenue for themselves. Issuing banknotes is like borrowing money for free. You accumulate more and more money without having to pay for it. Instead of banks paying interest to a person who deposited funds with them, they just printed a banknote, and – boom – they had more money. As long as their banknotes were accepted, it was a very good deal indeed.

Today, we take both banks and money for granted. They're just there, and they seem to have existed since time immemorial. That's probably a result of it being in all currency issuers' interest to create a sense of trust. Eternal trust. We just have to believe in those little pieces of paper. However, the story of Stockholms Banco, the first issuer of banknotes in Europe, shows that printing paper money is a fairly recent phenomenon in our part of the world.

There are three more interesting vignettes in the story of paper money in Sweden. The first is that Sweden was an early adopter of banknotes – the first country in Europe to do so. The same country that is now one of the first to phase out cash. The Kingdom of Sweden has probably progressed further than most other countries towards being a cashless society. The second thing to note is that all banks issue far more money than they hold as assets. That applies far beyond the dodgy Johan Palmstruch. The banks just need to make sure their customers have enough trust in them that they never make a run on the bank and try to withdraw all their money at once. The third interesting avenue of this little story is the way banks try to create trust in paper money.

For a long time, the value of banknotes was guaranteed by a certain quantity of gold held by a bank. It was simple and easy to grasp. The value of the notes could not just vanish into thin air. This easy-to-understand system acquired the somewhat more opaque name of the *gold standard*.

Many countries had a variant of that system at different times in the 19th and 20th centuries. For example, countries including France, Italy, Vatican City and Switzerland united to form the Latin Monetary Union in the 19th century. They pegged the value of their national currencies to a certain quantity of gold and a certain quantity of silver. The idea was that this would stabilise the value of both coins and paper money. As we have seen, everything depends on trust and faith in currencies and their value. But, as time went on, major discoveries of gold – including in the American gold rush – affected the value of gold in relation to the value of silver. Trust was eroded. And, if someone happened to discover a huge vein of silver on the other side of the world, the price of silver would crash. That would cause the system to wobble again.

Up in northern Europe, Sweden, Norway and Denmark formed a currency union in the 19th century. It was somewhat like the use of the euro in many countries across Europe. All three Scandinavian countries introduced the krona (plural: kronor) as their currency. They also agreed that one krona would be divided into 100 öre. The krona family was based on the gold standard, and the value of the krona was pegged to a certain quantity of gold. Sweden remained on the gold standard until 1931. If you get hold of a Swedish banknote from 1939, you will still see a line that says the Riksbank guarantees it will exchange the note for the equivalent value in gold. That was about building trust in paper money.

After Sweden left the gold standard behind, the value of the krona was pegged to the US dollar instead, in an international network known as the Bretton Woods system. Of course, trust and confidence continued to be just as important as before. Now, though, the means of creating trust was a bit different. Bretton Woods is a ski resort in the state of New Hampshire in the north-eastern United States. There, at the well-appointed Mount Washington Hotel, a group of the world's leading economists and politicians met for a conference in July 1944. The Allied forces had just made their D-Day landings in Normandy the previous month. Victory in the war against Germany and the Axis powers was near. Now, the economists met to draw up a new framework for the global economic system after the Second World War. Forty-four countries were represented at the conference. The group resolved to set up a body they dubbed the World Bank, as well as the International Monetary Fund (IMF). In three weeks of deliberations on the hotel's spacious verandas, in the conference rooms and on the golf courses, they also hammered out a new monetary system. Member countries would peg their own currencies at a fixed exchange rate to the dollar, the currency of the world's largest economy and the major power about to emerge victorious from the war. The value of the dollar, in turn, was based on – you guessed it – gold. America's gold was stored in the impenetrable vaults of Fort Knox. So, in a way, the gold standard still existed, via the dollar.

The reason for linking other currencies to the US dollar was to put a stop to the cause of problems occurring in global trade since the 1930s. In that decade, a number of countries had devalued their currencies in order to lower the prices of their own goods abroad, thereby boosting their exports. There were also strict limits, known as currency restrictions, on how much money people could take in and out of their own country. The economists at Bretton Woods thought those conditions were bad for trade and contributed to high unemployment in the various member countries. With the Great Depression of the 1930s and mass unemployment still fresh in their minds, the attendees of the Bretton Woods conference believed that such disruptions actually reduced living standards. The new system was designed to manage those problems.

Of course, the Bretton Woods system did not last for ever either. It remained in place until 1971, breaking up when the US could no longer guarantee it. The enormous cost of America's war in Vietnam was dragging the US economy down. Currency values began to float more or less freely. Not even a hint of a gold standard. By this time, we had taken another step away from the link between a unit of money and a certain quantity of a precious metal. No gold. No silver.

But, if we think about it, why is the value of gold or silver less symbolic than a piece of paper? It's equally made up. Gold is a very soft metal that does not have many uses other than for making jewellery. But it is shiny and beautiful. And we are used to thinking of gold as valuable. Nevertheless, its value is a construct. It is not useful. We can't eat gold. But, because everyone wants it, it still has value, even in spite of its short-comings as an object – especially when entire countries and regions are in flux. Gold is not dependent on the continued existence of a country, bank or currency.

There is an ancient Greek myth about king Midas, who had done a favour for the god Dionysus. In return, Midas was granted a wish. He wished that everything he touched would turn into gold. Delighted, he went round his garden and touched the trees and the roses. Everything was transformed into gold. His wish really had come true. He was thrilled. To mark the occasion, he ordered his servants to arrange a lavish feast. When he touched all the food and drink, they also turned to gold. In one version of the story, Midas's daughter comes home and is sad that the flowers have lost their colour and scent. To comfort her, Midas reaches out his hand, causing her to turn into – you guessed it – gold. He begs Dionysus to take away his talent – or curse. Midas is allowed to wash off his curse in Lydia's Pactolus River. The river's sandy bed is transformed into gold and electrum, or white gold – the same alloy that was used in the world's first coins by Lydia's real-life king Alyattes. He was the man with the stamp and the 168 grains of wheat.

When we think about money, most of us probably imagine a pile of banknotes and coins. That's how it has looked for the past several cen-turies: money is something you can touch. Or it was up until recently, anyway. Nowadays, we might also think of a credit card and some digits on a screen. But we still think they somehow represent piles of notes and coins.

New technology is now changing the monetary landscape. It is going to get harder to visualise those banknotes and coins, especially in Sweden. We are working hard to eliminate cash here. Not that long ago, Sweden's Riksbank updated the banknotes and coins with new designs that were meant to be much harder to counterfeit. The new banknotes bore portraits of Swedish stars like Greta Garbo and Ingmar Bergman, instead of old kings. Nice and modern. The bad news is that hardly anyone uses cash anymore. Paper money is used so rarely in Sweden that few people are able to distinguish genuine notes from forgeries. So the new banknotes are actually easy to fake, even if they are hard to copy in purely *technical* terms. Talk about wasted effort on the part of the Riksbank! The good news is that counterfeiting is not such a big deal. After all, hardly anyone uses cash, so there are few opportunities for forgers to get rich. That is one strong indication that we are moving away from our old banknotes and coins.

But, if money is not banknotes and coins anymore, what is it? It's clearly not gold, either. Or silver. We don't go round with spools of gold or silver wire; we put those behind us long ago. If money is just numbers on a screen, or on a bank statement, what actually is it? And where does it come from?

To find the answer, let's go to the bank. That's actually where money comes from. But it doesn't work in the way most people might think. A lot of people imagine that the bank simply gives out the same money savers previously paid in. That's essentially how a lot of economics textbooks explain it – if they even mention banks, that is. Many economic theories do not mention the role of banks. The banks just exist. They are outside the system, outside the *market*.

Here's how money is created today. You go to the bank and ask for a loan. Let's say you want to borrow a million to buy a house. The people at the bank assess your ability to pay. You are approved and sign an agreement. Then the banker enters 1,000,000 in their computer, and that amount is transferred to your account. This is where it happens. When you agree to owe money to the bank, an asset is created for the bank. They now have a claim on you, with your house as security. Hey presto! A million has now been added to the economy. The bank lent out money it didn't have. Or nearly didn't have. The bank has to have a certain amount of *real* capital, but the requirement is less than 10% in most countries. If you borrow 100 kronor, the bank has *made up* 92 of them – or maybe even a little more. The capital requirements for banks are a complicated story, where the banks themselves decide how risky a loan is and set the bar for their capital requirements themselves. Very convenient, if you happen to be a bank.

In a way, it leads back to Palmstruch's era once again, and to the late 19th century, when commercial banks printed their own banknotes. Today's banks have their own digital currency mints. Sweden's Riksbank and other central banks around the world have gradually lost their grip on the monetary supply. Now, private entities influence the supply of money that circulates. In many ways, the Riksbank is back where it was in 1903, prior to its monopoly on printing banknotes.

You already know Palmstruch and his predecessor, Kushim the book-keeper. Now you will meet some more figures, businessmen as well as bankers. We will finish up in contemporary homes, with your mortgage, your payment instalments, and our cashless society. But first we will travel back to where it all started – to the emergence of banks. Loans of various types have always existed, just as exchanges of objects have. In their simplest form, borrowing and lending have been around as long as human beings, though perhaps not always as formalised. In Babylonia, you could borrow seeds to sow; you would repay the loan from your harvest. In the Roman Empire, there were moneylenders, a simple banking system and loans with interest. When Christianity became established, interest was regarded as usury, so interest-bearing loans were out.

All three Abrahamic religions   Judaism, Christianity and Islam – have prohibitions against interest and usury. The rules against interest and usury – that is, making money on loans – differ between those faiths. Christians were forbidden to charge interest up until the Middle Ages. Christianity also frowns on *borrowing* money and being in debt. As long as the pope was in sole charge of the Christian Church, prior to the Reformation, his view of interest as a form of usury was the law. During that time, Christians relied on Jews when they needed to borrow money. Jews were forbidden to charge interest if they were lending to fellow Jews, but not if they were lending to Christians. For Muslims, interest was always forbidden. So religion determined the external framework for what was allowed or not. Merchants and everyone else had to obey the rules. Punishments were often severe.

As a result, Jewish families became the first bankers in Europe. Banking was born in medieval Europe. It became firmly established in the Lombardy region of northern Italy, in cities such as Florence and Siena.

The word 'bank' comes from Italian *il banco*, which referred to the benches in large market halls where farmers traded in grain, fabrics and other commodities. At that time, Jews could not own land, so they could not plant crops. Instead, they could lend money from their benches, using future crops as collateral. That was a very insecure form of collateral, since crops could fail. But the Jewish merchants could charge interest, because they were not subject to any ban on usury. They would also guarantee the supply of future harvests to purchasers – an early form of insurance. Eventually, some Jewish merchants came to specialise in these types of loans and insurance transactions. They were always to be found at *il banco*. They became bankers. Over time, they became the target of admiration, disgust and envy. People have a complicated attitude to money and wealth.

Depictions of these conflicting feelings can be found in the theatre. Shakespeare's play *The Merchant of Venice* captures the difficulty European Christianity had in dealing with questions concerning money. Loans and debts, wealth and interest are loaded subjects, to say the least. We still have mixed feelings about banks and money today, but in those days matters were even more highly charged with religion and religious sentiment. Shylock, the merchant in Shakespeare's play, is a Jew who lives in Venice's ghetto, the island where Jews were forced to live. Shylock is depicted as a greedy, vengeful man, who demands a pound of the borrower's flesh as security for a loan. But he also delivers an eloquent speech at his trial in which he attacks Christians' double standards. To borrow money while condemning the moneylender is a double standard, to put it mildly.

Solutions usually emerge to problems like this, especially if there's some money to be made. In order to get round the ban on interest, some real-life Christian merchants in Lombardy came up with a new idea. They would use three simultaneous contracts, thereby avoiding any violation of the lending rules. It went like this: say you want to borrow money for a business transaction, you would be offered three separate contracts. The first is a contract for someone to invest a sum in your business – what amounts to an interest-free loan. The loan becomes an investment. Then, the same person purchases an insurance agreement from you – an insurance policy. That deal represents the interest, but it is called an insurance payment. Finally, you get a third contract which states that you can keep any profit generated by the business transaction. Three contracts, known as *contractum triniu* in Latin, enabled Christians to get involved in the new finance industry. We will encounter clever financial vehicles throughout history. This is just the beginning.

So, in the 13th and 14th centuries, Christian Lombards entered the moneylending business, and this business expanded substantially in the Renaissance. Renaissance-era Italy still consisted of many smaller states. Florence had the Medici family, who were wool merchants. They would establish perhaps the most influential bank of all. They purchased fabric from the British Isles, from where it was transported to Florence to be made into other goods, which were then exported. The Medici were among the first to use a ledger book to keep track of their business transactions all over Europe. They recorded their transactions using a new technique known as double-entry bookkeeping. Each amount was entered in two places: as a debit and a credit. When the two columns were added up, they should total the same amount. If you study accounting today, you will learn the same method, which is still used by every company.

With their vast fortune, the Medici family became patrons to a long list of Renaissance artists, philosophers and scientists, including Leonardo da Vinci, Botticelli, Michelangelo, Donatello and Galileo Galilei. Without the Medici, the Renaissance would not have flourished the way it did. Under their influence, Florence became a place brimming with creativity in art, architecture and science. For several centuries, the city teemed with painters, sculptors and philosophers. Successful, wealthy business people and large numbers of talented people were drawn to the place where the present met the future – just like Amsterdam a few hundred years earlier, or Babylonia in the distant past.

The word 'renaissance' means rebirth. *Re-naissance.* The era marked the rebirth of faith in human ability and reason. The philosophy and knowledge from Ancient Greece and Rome were rediscovered. But this is where something remarkable happened. By looking back, people in the Renaissance began to look forward, towards the future. Something happened with our perception of time. That, in turn, paved the way for a couple of financial tools that would take on enormous importance – namely, loans and interest: two instruments that are crucial for rapid economic progress.

The idea of a 'golden age' was prevalent in the Middle Ages, up to the Renaissance. Everything was better in the past, so to speak – so things could only get worse. That mindset doesn't exactly spur people to invest in the future. The idea that things used to be better has been around for a long time. It is even present in the Bible. Adam and Eve lived in Paradise, then along came the serpent. They ate the apple, and then everything went downhill. Other cultures had similar myths. Once upon a time, the gods lived on Earth, or we lived alongside the gods, or under a wise, mythical ruler. Everything was wonderful in that golden age, but now everything is terrible. If things are just going to get worse, we might as well live now. Don't think about tomorrow. Medieval people had a very static view of the world. Nothing changed. Everything had its predetermined place. And people had their predetermined role in society. If you were born poor, it was God's will. You would stay poor, but be rewarded in heaven. If you were born a shoemaker, you would remain a shoemaker. Charging interest was regarded as a sin. There was a direct link to greed, one of the seven deadly sins.

When people began to idolise classical ideals and retranslate ancient texts, knowledge gradually began to spread. The notion took hold that our knowledge could build on that of previous generations. We could stand on those giants' shoulders, but we could also surpass them – with their help – so the world could advance, improve, make progress.

This mindset laid the foundations for the vast prosperity that industrialisation would later generate.

The Reformation in the 16th century split Christianity into Protestants in the north and Catholics in the south. Things started to loosen up in business and commerce. New shoots sprang up in the north, with more banks opening across Germany, the Netherlands and England. The Protestant work ethic took over. Put simply, interest was no longer a sin, but idleness was. People were supposed to work hard and live frugally – or at least appear to do so. Whatever you earned was not to be frittered away, but reinvested. This is the actual core of capitalism: reinvesting at least part of your profit, so that the capital can continue to grow. In that sense, Protestantism and capitalism go hand in hand. Some commentators even claim it's the reason the Industrial Revolution started in Europe.

So much for the history of banking. But what do banks actually do nowadays? Economics textbooks say that banks exist to lend money to people who want to start businesses, which in turn create jobs and growth. In actuality, that is just a small part of what banks do today. They also transmit payments. And, a lot of the time, they create money. Most of that money – nearly 80% – is spent on real estate. And most of those properties are not new constructions; they already exist. The result is that more money – which is being created all the time – is chasing a finite number of houses that are already built. Ka-ching. The price of housing goes up.

Banks have a tendency to create ever more money. Since the Second World War, the amount of money, or capital, in the Western world has increased far faster than our wages and faster than economic growth – every year, for decades. The total size of the economy has risen by around 5% annually since the 1950s, known as the post-war era; the monetary supply, or capital, has grown by 15% annually – three times as much. The conclusion is clear: we now receive more wages per person, which makes us feel richer. We have also grown richer on paper. The value of the houses we own goes up because there is more capital in circulation. This in turn fuels the banks. They see the collateral, the houses, going up in value, so they can lend more money – which they do by creating more money. That's how it continues.

Not all aspects of the system are entirely stable, though. Everything works until someone starts to doubt that value will continue to increase, because ultimately it's all about trust and confidence. If we lose confidence, the machine grinds to a halt.

But is borrowing more and more a bad system? It might be tempting to rush to that conclusion. Household borrowing in advanced economies went from the equivalent of 50% of GDP around 1950 to 170% in 2007. We're up to our eyeballs in debt.

What's good about your loans is that if – but only *if* – you borrow for the right things, you actually do get richer. And you will get richer a lot faster than if you had tried to earn the same amount just by working. Often, a loan is required in order to earn that money in the first place. You can think of the loan as a sort of tool.

Debts – or, more precisely, loans – can act like a long lever. If you make more on your business deal than the interest you pay on the loan, you end up with a profit. Banks work in the same way in the textbook sense. They take in money at a certain interest rate, which they pay to savers. They lend money at a higher interest rate. The difference is called the net interest-rate spread. You also need a positive net interest-rate spread in your own deals. If you borrow to purchase something that will generate income for you – preferably ongoing income – that's good. For example, if you take out a loan to buy a house you can rent out, some land to grow food, or a shop where you can sell things – all of those can potentially be good reasons for getting into debt. You can earn more than the interest and payments on the loan, so over time you can pay off your debt. At the end, you will have achieved an income at a level you couldn't have had before. And you will also own an asset in the form of a house, a piece of land or a shop. The loan proved to be a good deal for the borrower – a good deal for you.

The downside of loans, from your personal perspective, is when you borrow for consumption, though it can be good for others, such as the people who sell what you consume and society as a whole. But it's not so good for you. You consume the money you borrowed, and then you're left with only your debt. Or maybe you misjudged your business deal. You didn't manage to rent out the house you bought because a pandemic grounded all air travel. The crop on your land failed. Your shop wasn't as popular as you had hoped and your merchandise remained unsold. Now, you're in debt. Not good. The lever has moved in the other direction.

Our homes and mortgages are really a chapter all on their own. For many people, borrowing to buy a home is the biggest purchase they'll make in their life. In recent decades in Sweden, borrowing up to your eyeballs and buying the most expensive home you can get has been a surprisingly good move. Prices have kept going up and up. But property markets have crashed in the past. The last time it happened on a large scale was in 2008. It started with sub-prime mortgages in the USA and spread from there around the whole world.

Swedish banks are regarded as particularly solvent, with their 8% capital. Other banks might have 3%. Prior to the 2008 financial crisis, banks held even less capital. Bank capital is important in two ways. If a bank has a lot of its own money compared to what it lends, the bank is highly stable – but less profitable. Why is that? Well, it's because profit is expressed as a percentage of assets. So, how much do you earn on the money you've actually invested? Let's say you need 1,000 euros to do a deal. You have only 100 euros. You can borrow 900 euros with interest. After the deal, you have to deduct the interest. But let's say you would have made a total profit of 50 euros on the deal. You've made a 50% profit on the money you invested; that is, on your own equity. That's good. The less of your own capital you have to invest, the better your profit in percentage terms, all other things being equal. So, if you only needed to invest 50 euros of your own capital instead of 100, and you still earned 50 euros, you'd make 100% profit. That's why it's profitable to have as little of your own capital, or equity, as possible.

The calculations above explain the origin of the process that led to the failure of Lehman Brothers, a long-established investment bank, in 2008, which set off the financial crisis that shook the world. Lehman Brothers had issued $680 billion (!) in loans, but had only $22.5 billion in assets. That's around 3%. So, if prices fell by between 3% and 5%, all their capital would be wiped out. To cap it all, they had specialised in a category of mortgages called *sub-prime*. As the name indicates, these were bad loans, with a high risk that the borrowers would be unable to pay off their debts. Put simply, the bank's customers had equally narrow margins in their finances as the bank itself. Once doubt set in, the snow-ball started to build. Trust evaporated. Lehman Brothers went bust. The same thing can happen in times of instability, such as during a war or crisis. Sometimes a bank's customers make a run on a bank, all rushing to withdraw their money at the same time. That happened when the rouble collapsed after Russia's invasion of Ukraine in the spring of 2022 and the Western world imposed economic sanctions against Russia. Russians tried to withdraw their savings. Of course, the money did not exist. The authorities responded by shutting down cash machines and restricting banks' opening hours. That postponed the problem. In such cases, it might be possible to rebuild some trust and dissuade some people from withdrawing their money. It is worth noting here that there are also differences between banks. Old-fashioned local savings banks are much more solvent than Lehman Brothers was. They have a capital adequacy ratio of 15% or more. That's about the same as the requirement for mortgage applicants in Sweden, who need a deposit of 15%. Otherwise lenders regard them as too risky.

The 2008 financial crisis led to extremely low interest rates. They were intended as a short-term measure, but remained in effect far longer than any financial expert could have anticipated. Few people predicted that the world would live with interest rates close to zero for more than a decade. Low interest rates have created the prevailing economic climate during this time. Have conditions been mild and pleasant, or overheated and feverish? In any event, it's very, very unusual, and the world has not seen such low interest rates in 5,000 years – not since Babylonian times, when Kushim the beer-drinking bookkeeper inscribed cuneiform figures on his clay tablets. Negative interest rates – that is, percentages below zero – have never been seen before. There have been religious prohibitions on charging interest, but interest rates have never been negative.

Just imagine getting paid to take out a loan.

A GLOBAL BRING-YOUR-OWN PARTY

In which the ape closes some gates and opens others, then starts exchanging things with the whole world.

THE BRAIN IS WHERE IT HAPPENS.
Great revolutions play out just behind the forehead.

No technical or scientific breakthroughs are needed to start exchanging things, instead of trying to make everything yourself. It doesn't require any sophisticated equipment either. All it takes is a little thought. An idea. One day, two apes discovered they could use simple means to become a little better off. But, despite its simplicity, that idea has influenced the course of world events for hundreds of thousands of years. It has also been a part of the formation of what we call the Nordic model of social welfare.

Money did not entail or require any technical innovation. Like bartering, money originated from an idea – an idea that has played a role in shaping the world we know today.

Over time, our planet has been transformed into a single, huge, spinning marketplace. In just a short time – indeed, just a few hundred years – we have made our home in the cosmos into one large, pulsating bazaar, a place where we exchange things with one another left and right, 24/7, across every imaginable boundary. Just imagine all the shopping malls around the world, the stock-market trading and the booming Internet commerce that goes on round the clock.

Paying for things with money was one of the big ideas behind today's global commerce – a condition for large-scale exchange. The other big idea, the impact of which has become clear in hindsight, is the elimination of measures that hinder or prevent trading. In purely practical terms, this has often meant refraining from collecting tariffs at the first opportunity.

The idea of imposing some sort of fee – a customs charge – on passing merchants has followed humanity throughout history. Such charges are an appealingly simple, reliable source of revenue for those with strong arms and a sharp sword. Or perhaps access to a small army. Customs charges, or tolls, have often determined the location and layout of our cities. In many cases, the best military position for a city coincided with the best place to extract tolls. Stockholm is a brilliant example of this, as it was founded on an island where Lake Mälaren flows into the Baltic Sea. If you controlled that little granite rock, you could control all trade between Lake Mälaren and the Baltic, and therefore the rest of the world. Plus, you could charge customs fees.

Nowadays, the term 'toll barrier' is usually used figuratively in the business press and political discourse. But, for thousands of years, actual toll gates were a real presence in people's lives. It seems obvious to us today that we shouldn't have to pay tolls or customs charges to trade between cities and places in our own country – or even within the EU. But things were not always like that. Not at all. You had to pay a toll in order to gain access to a city's market square. In the Middle Ages, and even earlier, European cities were enclosed by city walls. The barriers were clear and tangible. Consider the Brandenburg Gate, the last remaining city gate from Berlin's toll barrier. An even clearer example is the solid stone wall that still surrounds the town of Visby on the Swedish island of Gotland, a major trading centre in medieval times.

The rules were simple. You had to pay to come in and trade. If you lived inside the city walls, you had certain rights. Some tradespeople might be authorised to produce specific goods and sell them. Sweden's great 17th-century warrior king, Gustavus Adolphus, like all wartime leaders, needed all the sources of income he could get. He declared a ban on all trading outside of towns and cities. If farmers wanted to sell their produce, they had to go to the market in town. That system remained in force in Sweden for several hundred years, up to 1810. Stockholm was surrounded by a fence, with gates at certain places. Those were the only points through which you could bring goods into the city. A relic of that era lives on in Stockholm, where the residents talk about living 'inside the toll gates,' meaning in the centre, or 'outside the toll gates.' The city centre was like the duty-free shop in a major airport: big crowds waiting to get in, but, once you were inside, a fragrant and far nicer place opened up. A separate little world. Even today, living in

Stockholm's historic centre 'inside the toll gates' is more prestigious than living further out.

How did toll gates affect the functioning of the economy? And how did they affect cities? We can look at some other examples around the world. In Paris, the toll gates remained in place longer than in Stockholm. When Baron Haussmann modernised Paris in the mid-19th century, designing wide boulevards, parks, monuments, a sewer system and a water-supply system to bring clean drinking water into the city, he ran short of money. It costs money to build all those things. He chose to finance his infrastructure by raising the city toll, known as *l'octroi*. The city walls were long gone. Instead, a fence was built around the city perimeter. Of course, long queues of horses, wagons and carts formed at the gates, where all goods were subject to customs charges. People could enter toll-free, but tolls had to be paid for all goods brought in. The queues were a major problem, affecting both rich and poor. When upper-class Parisians' carriages headed out to the Bois de Boulogne, a pleasant new park, they had to queue at the checkpoint near the Arc de Triomphe.

Parisian tariffs had other effects too. Just outside the city's perimeter fence, where goods could be brought without charge, new factories and workshops sprang up like mushrooms. Paris was surrounded by a ring of flourishing industries, like the rings of Saturn. The outer edge of the city, just inside the fence, remained green and undeveloped because of the tolls. Haussmann took the view that the industrialists were benefiting from the new streets, the sewer, clean drinking water, pleasant parks and new theatres, so they should pay their way. After much debate, the toll fence was moved further out. Paris swallowed up a number of its surrounding municipalities. Eventually, internal tariffs were removed within France, and the customs boundary ended up at the national border. A larger market, less crowding and more trade. In the latter half of the 20th century, France's customs area was expanded again when it joined the European Economic Community. Now, the fence is at the EU border.

Creating large markets – such as the present-day European Union – and trading at all times, with everyone, as if there were no borders, is actually another idea that has grown into a vast machine. Instead of manufacturing, growing or trading things at home, we think bigger. Much bigger. Nowadays, we often think in terms of the whole planet – going global.

And thinking big is exactly what we humans started to do, more than ever. The music world, sport, science and commerce – everybody has been at it. Especially in the last 30 to 40 years. Thanks to new technology and more open borders, the advantages of a large market are available to everyone. Exchanging things was the first idea that set the wheels in motion. Today, we know it is applicable to nearly every domain: science, culture and sport have all taken up the idea of cross-border exchange.

The concept is as simple as it is broad. Every country, culture or region around the world contributes what it is good at in an increasingly open world. Goods or knowledge. A sort of global bring-your-own party. China serves as the world's workshop and factory. The US handles computing and maintenance. London is the world's financial centre – or at least was, before Brexit. Norway brings the salmon. And little Sweden has trucks and pop music. Then, everyone buys and sells with everyone else.

We probably wouldn't have become this globalised without early traders' expeditions. People on different continents would hardly know of each other's existence. Trade has spurred explorers to travel across the globe. The desire to exchange goods, the opportunities to earn piles of money, plus our natural curiosity, have pushed us to take enormous risks, time and time again. By venturing to try something nobody had done before, people discovered and mapped new parts of the world.

Spices were something that attracted us all over the world: an appealing item with a high exchange value, and relatively easy to transport – they were, in other words, possessed of the best possible characteristics for those interested in trade.

Christopher Columbus was one such person. Born in Genoa, a rival to the city state of Venice, he spent many years in Lisbon before approaching the king of Spain for patronage in 1492. He was a man with a plan. When Columbus set sail *westwards* across the Atlantic, he was searching for a sea route to India – which is located *east* of Europe. However, knowing that the Earth is round, he correctly assumed he would eventually reach

India if he just kept heading far enough west. Once in India, he planned to acquire spices and gold, and perhaps launch a little holy war in honour of the king and queen of Spain. When he reached some islands that he thought belonged to India, he mistakenly dubbed them the West Indies. We still call them by that name today. The indigenous people of the Americas are no longer called Indians, though.

Why was it so important to find a new route to India? At that time, trade with Asia was dominated by the city state of Venice and the Ottoman Empire. The Ottomans had conquered Constantinople in 1453. They had also had the cheek to impose tariffs. Yes, toll barriers again. And Venice was trying to secure a monopoly on trade with the East. We don't like monopolies – especially if others control them. The Venetians colluded with the Ottomans, who controlled the Silk Road, the overland trade route connecting Europe, India and China. Traders everywhere from Genoa to Lisbon were annoyed. The Silk Road happens to be the same route China's current leadership under President Xi Jinping wants to resurrect with the huge 'Belt and Road' project. China's thoughts and actions today echo those of the Spanish and Portuguese in the 15th century. You can go a long way with your own trade routes and your own ports in strategic locations. Some ideas stick around.

Unfortunately, Columbus did not find any spices in his West Indies. However, the Portuguese explorer Vasco da Gama had better luck when he sailed in the opposite direction a few years later. With great difficulty, he managed to sail round the southern tip of Africa, becoming the first European to do so. With the help of an Arab navigator he had picked up in a West African port, da Gama sailed his ship across the Indian Ocean to Malabar, the Spice Coast. He reached the centre of the spice trade. Jackpot!

When Vasco da Gama returned to Lisbon in 1499, he had lost several ships and half his crew. But the spices and fabrics he brought back from Malabar paid off the expedition's costs six times over. It was an undisputed success. He set about planning a new expedition, and he was not alone. The Spanish, French, Dutch and English rushed to follow. There was a race for spices, fabrics, gold and other commodities. The Portuguese occupied the port of Goa, north of the Malabar Coast, and this tactic became part of a pattern that was repeated by the Portuguese and other European nations.

Why did we apes do all this?

What is so magically tempting about cinnamon, ginger, cardamom and pepper? Pepper in particular seems to have magical properties. Of course, the reason is that European food is so much tastier with the addition of spices. Spices add a totally new aroma to dishes. To a large extent, that was the impetus for explorers' voyages. The taste of spices was something people were willing to pay a fortune for. Apes like to eat tasty food and are prepared to pay a good price for it – a very good price indeed.

The taste of spices was so special that it also lent status and honour to those who acted as hosts and could offer that sensory experience to their guests. In turn, that raised the price of spices even further, which then made new trade voyages even more profitable. As we saw earlier, spices are a particularly good commodity for a number of reasons. They weigh little in relation to their value, and most spices can be transported over long distances with no detriment to quality.

Somewhere around here we can really start to talk about true global trade. We were discovering ever more of the world. A few centuries later, colonialism would take hold, along with the slave trade. The network between Africa, Europe and America was known as the triangular slave trade. Instead of goods, it dealt in people on one leg of the route. The people were captured and transported as slaves from West Africa to the West Indies, North and South America. Many perished en route. Sugar, cotton and tobacco were shipped from the New World plantations to Europe. From Europe, ships took fabrics and liquor to West Africa. It was a horrific chapter in the history of trading.

When slavery was abolished in the 19th century, global trade expanded in scope. This was due to three ideas that arose around the same time. Each idea was very powerful in its own right, but together their effects were multiplied. The world was embarking on two centuries that would give rise to greater change, wealth and catastrophe than humanity had ever experienced before. This was the dawn of the industrial age.

The first idea was industrial-scale specialisation. The conveyor belt.

Factory workers focused on a single task and became extremely skilled at that task. The tasks were monotonous and in many cases extremely inhumane, but terribly efficient in terms of production.

The second idea was to utilise coal-fired steam engines. These two ideas helped Britain to become a leading economic power.

The third idea was related to our good old tariff barriers. If you want to make trading easier, it can help to have fewer tariffs. The idea that tariffs were a bad thing first took hold in Britain. Customs charges made trading less appealing. Yet, as we have seen, exchanging things is beneficial for both parties. So, the more things that are traded, the better – for everyone involved. But that means we have to get rid of as many of the obstacles as possible that prevent us from travelling, meeting and exchanging things with one another. Walls of all kinds need to be torn down – including all the various border checks, charges and gates along the way. And the fewer customs charges imposed, the more trade there will be. And the more trade, the better for both parties, as long as both benefit from the transaction. Thus the idea of what became known as free trade was born.

Free trade was riding high in the second half of the 19th century. The world was experiencing a wave of globalisation, which had many similarities to the wave we have seen in recent decades. People were living in a more open world, powered by the engine of trade. Then came the backlash. Nationalism gained traction and took on new overtones. Calls were made for new tariffs: 'We want to protect what's ours.' It all came to a screeching halt in 1914. The First and Second World Wars transformed the world into a melange of nations and states with closely guarded borders – the worst possible conditions for free trade. Not until the end of the Second World War did the world gradually start to open up again.

Global trade has gone through waves of increased and decreased openness. After living in a more open world of increasing prosperity for everyone, where walls are torn down and border checks vanish, the outbreak of war, or someone's perception that things are too open, leads us to think we aren't better off at all and are just being tricked by everyone else – others, who are taking our jobs. And so the world starts to build new walls. Or fences. But, as we shall see, we do seem to be moving in a particular direction, especially when we look at things in the long term. Despite all the setbacks, wars and crises, we are now – in the early 21st century – cooperating across national borders more than ever before.

But the direction of progress is never a given. Whether you build walls or ships, that is always a choice. The story of Zheng He, a Chinese admiral largely unknown in the West, exemplifies just how different our image of the world might have looked.

Fully 85 years before Columbus discovered America, the Chinese admiral sailed westward. He undertook a series of overseas expeditions on a far greater scale than anything the Portuguese, Spanish, English or Dutch could have achieved. He totally outstripped them. Columbus had three ships, the largest of which was a three-masted vessel. Zheng He had 300 vessels, and his largest ship had nine masts; his fleet was crewed by 27,000 men – an astounding number, when compared to European figures. They criss-crossed the Indian Ocean on seven expeditions, visiting Mecca, Mombasa, Sri Lanka, India and Indonesia. After Zheng He's death in 1435, and then the death of the emperor, everything changed. The new emperor decided to pour all the Empire's resources into building – you guessed it – a wall. To keep the Mongols out. *Build the Wall*. No more ships. Instead, we got the Great Wall of China – the exact opposite of openness and exchange. The new emperor even went so far as to ban the construction of large ships. China ceased to be a maritime power. As is so often the case, things really could have turned out differently.

If the world long ago resembled a colourful patchwork of tribes and regions, it is now starting to look more like a monochrome painting. Local celebrities mingle with global stars everywhere. We trade with one another. We talk to one another. We play with one another. Wherever, whenever. Everything from sport and culture to music and COVID-19 research is included. Come along to the global bring-your-own party. ABBA, Lady Gaga, Apple and CNN will get out there first and show the way. Develop a skill – any skill – and share it with the world.

Even grief can be shared globally. When Britain's Princess Diana died in a terrible car crash in Paris in 1997, the whole world grieved. To many,

many people, it felt as if they had lost someone they knew. Perhaps it's not so strange, when images and words had been cabled out across the world, weaving a modern tale of a beautiful but unhappy princess and her uncaring prince.

The starting shot for our latest round of globalisation was fired when China tentatively opened its doors to the rest of the world in the early 1980s. The world *globalisation* started to gain currency around that time. We went from a level of world trade that had been ticking along for some time, to another, *more intense* level. With the fall of the Berlin Wall in 1989 and then the break-up of the Soviet Union, barriers were being pulled down both literally and figuratively. A wave of opening up, deregulation and lower tariffs swept through the world. More countries embraced free trade. The vast nations of India and China opened up to the rest of the world. This is when China became 'the world's factory floor.'

Initially, Chinese factories produced simple products of often dubious quality. As the years passed, China's manufacturing became more advanced, and even high-tech in some sectors. Then, the Central Committee of the Chinese Communist Party decided to launch an experiment around some towns and fishing villages near the Pearl River Delta, not far from Hong Kong and Macao. That was in 1980, in a place called Shenzhen. The town of Shenzhen had a population of 25,000, with a few hundred thousand in the surrounding region. A free-trade zone was established there, free from nearly all the usual Communist rules, surrounded by a barbed-wire fence with checkpoints – a bit like the fence around 19th-century Paris, but with the factories on the inside rather than the outside. It worked. The city grew exponentially. By 2020, it had a population of 17.5 million. So, if we had to choose a single place to symbolise globalisation in its modern form, could it be Shenzhen?

The idea of doing away with toll barriers and borders swept around the world in the decades following the fall of the Berlin Wall. European leaders were devoted to the cause. The European Coal and Steel Union, founded in the 1950s by former enemies convinced that trade would promote peace, sensed victory in the 1990s. Communism had been defeated; capitalism was victorious. Some even spoke of the 'end of history.'

The European Common Market was implemented, with freedom of movement for goods, services, labour and capital: the four freedoms. The European Union acquired more member states, increasing the count from the six founder members to 27. The EU's single market expanded, making it easier to exchange things within Europe with no customs charges. Practices that were unthinkable just a few decades ago became part of daily life. Europeans also introduced a single currency, the euro, in 1999. Events seemed to be moving in one direction: lower tariffs, more trade and free movement for workers. The rest of the world looked at the European internal market and created similar joint projects – in North America, South America, Asia and Africa: regional internal markets. Billions of people were lifted out of poverty as small nations were linked up with the planet's immense trading mechanism. Today, everyone is involved and brings what they can to the party.

Sometimes, the whole trading mechanism comes in for criticism. Is the world really going to become a single, vast market? If so, what about countries' sovereignty? Is it really sensible to let our desire to trade with one another determine so much in our lives? Just look at wages around the world. There are winners as well as losers. Globalisation has evened out pay levels across the globe. Wages in the least developed countries have been boosted, at least if we look at the number of people who are better off. China and India are often used as examples of this. The proportion of people living in poverty in these two vast nations has decreased dramatically. We have seen similar economic development in many other countries too.

There is no doubt that conditions in factories in low-cost countries are deeply inhumane. Positively miserable. Nevertheless, these underpaid workers from rural areas have achieved better living conditions as factory workers in the global mechanism. Living standards and working conditions have gradually improved over the years. Developing countries and their people have grown significantly wealthier overall. This is social mobility on a global scale. But not everyone has moved up the ladder.

Over time, large-scale manufacturing of countless products has been offshored from Western factories to low-wage countries. Consequences for Western businesses and workers have often been severe – including unemployment, stagnating wages, or the need to take on low-paid work to make ends meet. When the 2008 banking crisis hit, previously faint resistance to the idea of a single global marketplace grew into vocal protests, especially in wealthy parts of the world. Apparently not everyone felt things were getting better. Fences, walls, barriers and obstacles came back into fashion in some circles. Various shades of antiglobalists made their voices heard. Once again, in the new millennium, we have heard political voices from the USA shouting 'America first.' In Europe, the UK took a clear step away from the common market by leaving the European Union. There's a snag in the global machinery. The idea of uniting the world in one big party has been questioned before. Just like in our own lives, big parties can often be chaotic and difficult to control. That's why the notion of leaving the party and regaining control of transactions keeps resurfacing from time to time. But the cost of leaving the party entirely has usually proved to be too high, even for large countries like the USA.

So the idea of the bring-your-own party has outlasted all the objections so far. If we look at the past century, the last forty years were a bonanza for trade and commerce. Everything that could be shipped was shipped, this way and that. Babies' dummies and oil. Salmon and lipstick. Music and food. The 21st century is a time unlike any other in our history. Commerce is on an unprecedented scale. Our world has become a village where everyone wants to exchange goods with everyone else. It is a world more open than ever. We're enjoying longer lifespans than ever, and there's less poverty – for more people than ever.

What a party!

But a little uninvited guest – who nobody had heard of before – put a stop to the global party in the spring of 2020. The novel coronavirus spread from country to country, causing a disease known as COVID-19. Economies came to an emergency stop. Borders were closed. Aircraft stayed on the ground. Two years later – just as the virus was loosening its grip on the world – Russia invaded Europe's next-largest nation by area. Ukraine became a war zone, with thousands of people dead and injured, and millions of refugees. Sanctions and fighting strangled food and energy supplies. After 40 years, the global trading party is over. For the time being, anyway.

Suddenly, having a super-specialised factory in Indonesia that manufactures face masks for the whole world seems stupid. A week-long yoga course in Bali feels dangerous. The dream of walking along the Great Wall of China has turned into a nightmare. And the ultra-modern German frozen pizza, with onions from Spain, peppers from Hungary and meat from Argentina, assembled in the Netherlands and then freighted to every country in the EU, suddenly feels *extremely* wrong. Once again, cracks are showing in the concept of our planet as one open marketplace, where almost everybody meets and exchanges things.

A MAGICAL MECHANISM

In which we meet the
moral philosopher Adam Smith
and see our ape transformed into
Scrooge McDuck – and learn why
the invisible hand needs rules
in order to work properly.

Magical, because it can transform some of the ugliest, lowest parts of our humanity – namely, egotism and self-interest – into something that benefits another person. And we still haven't managed to find another mechanism that can perform this trick anywhere near as well. But how exactly does it transform rubbish into the best thing there is? Some analogies and stories can help to explain.

We originated in the primordial soup. That's what biologists will tell you, anyway. It was a sort of gunge, where molecules started reproducing for some reason. After several billion years, the ape who was our ancestor bubbled up from the soup. Over time, every molecule and cell has ended up in the right place in our no-longer-quite-so-hairy bodies. Amazing, but true. It's about as amazing as the fact that all the loaves of bread baked around the world tonight will be on their way to their destinations in just a few hours. And – perhaps even more mind-blowing – in roughly the right quantities. The remarkable thing is that both the quantity and kind of bread are correct. Some magical mechanism ensures that the loaves of bread are not only baked, but also end up on the right breakfast tables, in supermarkets or hotel buffets.

Every night, a white-uniformed multinational army of bakers march to their kitchens. Dough is baked into bread. Then, a gigantic system of sales, packaging and transport swings into gear to make sure the right bread ends up in the right place, in roughly the right quantity and for a reasonable price. A vast array of people, thoughts and actions produce the same results every morning: namely, that there is reasonably priced bread in approximately the right place.

Adam Smith, an 18th-century Scotsman who came to be known as the first economist, termed this almost supernatural organisational ability 'the invisible hand.' With no visible manager in charge of global bread-baking, the appropriate amount of bread is made. And, most important of all, Smith notes that the bread on our table is not the result of bakers' great love for their fellow humans. Instead, it is the bakers' desire to do something for themselves or their families – their *self-interest* – that is transformed into something tasty for the rest of us. Similarly, musicians' own interest in playing guitar or singing is transformed into something we can all enjoy at a concert. Their self-interest becomes a source of enjoyment for others.

Here, too, the world can be viewed and interpreted in different ways. Things are often easier to understand if you look at them from multiple angles. Maybe we can catch sight of that invisible hand, or parts of it, if we poke around a bit more.

We can view the world as a mass of individuals, all of whom are preoccupied with their own lives. They all have a desire to create the best possible life for themselves. Somehow, their efforts to benefit themselves are then transformed into something that benefits others. Millions upon millions of people around the world, at slightly different times, all acting on their own, with no direction from above, and in their own interest, devote part or all of their days to something that gives them pleasure in their lives. Some people bake. Others sing or conduct research. The results of their efforts are often down-to-earth and con-crete. The hand may be invisible, but the results of that invisible hand are very visible. It may be a song, a meal or whatever someone felt like making. Then, they all come together – willingly or not – in a sort of talent show. Whose bread is the tastiest? Who's the best singer? Who has the best restaurant? Most of what we humans create and produce can be compared to the things other people make and do – objects or services of various kinds. This eternal talent show is usually called *competition*. Over time, those who are especially good at what they do are distinguished from those who are less good. And now we suddenly have two kinds of baker: good bakers and bad bakers. But this is not a self-help book for bakers or musicians. Their lives and their efforts to achieve a good life are no doubt fascinating, but our musicians and bakers are just examples to illustrate a bigger concept. What we have described is a gigantic mechanism, or principle, that actually holds true in most spheres of activity. We can think of it as the beating heart that makes a market economy function.

Adam Smith, the man with the invisible hand, was a philosopher – a moral philosopher. He studied human nature. What makes us act in a certain way? How can self-interest and egotism lead to something that benefits the general public? Morality has often accompanied economics throughout history. Gold and guilt.

As one of the first examples in his seminal book *The Wealth of Nations*, Smith described a small pin-making workshop. If an inexperienced person tried to make a pin, it would take them a whole day. Once that person had gained some experience, they might be able to produce 20 pins a day. But, by allocating specific tasks to different people who each specialise in their own part of the process, Smith showed how ten people in a blacksmith's workshop could produce a whopping 48,000 pins a day. The cost of producing 20 pins, in terms of man-hours, goes from a whole day for an experienced craftsman working alone to 1/240 of a day. That's a big difference in daily productivity, to put it mildly.

As you will have noticed, Adam Smith's pin workshop is based on the same magic as bartering – the activity we described (with only slight exaggeration) as making something out of thin air. The only thing that's added is an idea; everything else is the same. In our example with the apes, the nuts and figs just changed place, and suddenly both apes were better off. In Adam Smith's pin workshop, the work process is simply reallocated, and – hey presto – many more pins can be made in the same time. By *organising* their work differently, more value – pins – can be created from the same amount of material and the same number of workers. This happens because each worker's skill level increases, and they save time by not swapping between different tasks. In addition, it is economical to purchase specialised tools and machines that can further increase production. This is clearly an example written by a Scotsman at the start of the Industrial Revolution; he was amazed at the changing work practices he had started to notice, and at the surprising results the changes brought about.

If we may be wise after the fact, we can note that, as more pins are fabricated, more metal is consumed. As production increases, so does the consumption of natural resources. But that is a problem Adam Smith and his contemporaries could ignore. For them, the planet was infinite in comparison to the global population. Vast quantities of ore were available. Rubbish could be disposed of in the environment. One might as well tip a bucket of toxic waste into the sea, where it would be diluted and eventually disappear; given the size of the sea, it would be all right. We will return to this attitude to the Earth and its natural resources in later chapters. In Smith's day, people were more concerned about how to feed a growing population than about environmental issues.

Let's turn to another little detail of old Adam Smith's story that is often ignored. With every increase in specialisation, something important happens. As we refine and allocate work tasks among ourselves, we also have to get better at cooperating. That might mean cooperating with co-workers in a factory or with other people outside your company. The more we specialise, the more people are involved in making something like a shoe or a pin – it is an inevitable consequence of dividing up tasks. Smith noted that there are two ways of increasing specialisation and division of labour: by expanding the market or making the market more efficient. In a market of a given size – on an island, for example – we can utilise communications and transport to make the market work better. We have to be in contact in order to cooperate and specialise, and we need to be able to send items to and from various factories. Then, with increased division of labour and cooperation, we can create value. Thus size and specialisation are interrelated. The bigger the market, the more specialisation. But specialisation requires that we get along and cooperate. No fighting. We will see later on the importance of cooperation when we venture out into the world and exchange things with other countries and cultures. If we get along and exchange things peacefully with one another, everyone will benefit in the long run. If we start fighting, the markets will shrink and there will be less opportunity to specialise.

So, we need to specialise if we don't want to end up doing everything ourselves. The value of cooperation is surprisingly high. At the same time, we – or, more accurately, our self-interests – are in competition. This struggle of competing interests is in progress all over the world. We're involved, whether consciously or unconsciously. And we are being compared against others. Who has the best bread? Who's the best musician?

Chefs and farmers, architects and carpenters, publishers and authors – everyone is involved, whether they want to be or not, and everything can be categorised. Two piles: good and bad. It doesn't matter whether you're talking about a physical object – for example, a sack of potatoes or a mobile phone – or a service, like a massage.

The rest of us are the competition judges. Our votes in these talent competitions decide the results. Perhaps calling it a talent competition is taking it too far, but we do choose what we want to acquire in all the world's marketplaces. We also choose who we want to trade with and on what terms. The practicalities are a bit different, depending on the goods or services we're interested in. If we're talking music, then it's which concerts we choose to go to, how much we're willing to pay and which tracks we choose to download or listen to. If we're interested in restaurants and food, it's simply a matter of which place attracts the most customers.

The winner is determined by the sum total of the conditions. There are no permanent winners. Time and place will influence which of the the competing self-interests are rewarded and which are not. But the mechanism is always the same everywhere. The less good competitors are forgotten. Fewer people choose them. They fade away, while the good competitors are rewarded. Many people want to trade with them. The conditions keep improving. This is when profits can be made.

As Adam Smith acknowledged, self-interest is really not the same as egotism or evil. The term 'self-interest' has probably contributed to the frequent association of economics with our worst aspects. Humans have an instinctive dislike of selfish people. It is thought to be an inherited, even genetic, instinct. We know – often from experience – that selfish people are harmful to the group, or to society. This paradox fascinated Adam Smith. How can *self-interest*, which we intuitively recognise as bad, cumulatively lead to positive effects on the *public interest*? It's important to keep these concepts clear in our mind. One key nuance is that *self-interest* is not the opposite of *kindness*. Self-interest is not the same as *meanness* or *evil*. In the sense that Adam Smith uses it, self-interest always includes a sort of give-and-take. I need you and you need me. It takes two to tango, so to speak. As we have seen, both manufacturing and business are dependent on agreements and cooperation. There has to be someone to trade with, right?

This is one aspect that makes the market economy such a good fit. You could even go so far as to say that the economy is just another word for the human love of cooperating in clever ways. We don't run a bakery just to be nice to our fellow citizens – that would be a charity, and no doubt a wonderful service in the short term, but we'd go broke very quickly, and then our neighbours wouldn't have a bakery. But we don't run a bakery to be mean to others either. Our intention is not to trick or harm them. That sort of bakery wouldn't last long in our neighbourhood. Instead, we operate our bakery out of a sort of self-interest. We want to make a living by selling something we're good at making – namely, bread. The bread has to be good enough and reasonably priced, so that people prefer to buy it over baking their own. Anyone who's baked bread at home knows it takes a lot of time, practically half a day. It's hard to do another task while you're making lunch and working in the vegetable garden, and so on. Time to divide up the tasks: you bake, and I garden. Once again, specialising and exchanging goods looks like a brilliant idea.

There is one special type of division of labour we haven't talked about yet: that of the division of labour between men and women. It exists in every society and throughout history, even in hunter-gatherer cultures. The men hunt. The women gather. Men and women usually do different tasks in agricultural societies as well. The exact tasks vary from place to place, but they generally differ for men and women. Women often work in the fields, planting and harvesting, in addition to doing various crafts at home, such as weaving, sewing, making crockery and cooking. One interesting phenomenon is that, when these tasks are taken out of the darkness of the home into the light of a public setting, they often transfer from the female sphere to the male. A cook becomes a chef. A seamstress becomes a tailor. A wood-gatherer becomes a wood merchant. These tasks enter the economy.

Another example is health and social care. In many cultures, the work of looking after children and the elderly at home has traditionally been allocated to women, which has contributed to their invisibility in economic history and economic analyses. Thus women are relatively invisible in this book as well. Classical and neoclassical economics sees people as rational actors: *Homo economicus*, consumers or producers. But, if you look after a relative such as a child or parent, that activity is invisible because you are neither consuming nor producing. As the American economist Paul Samuelson put it, 'GDP will fall when a man marries his maid.'

Unpaid work is not counted as productive labour. It is not official-ly part of the economy. If no one pays you and you do not pay anyone else, you are not an economic actor. You are not a *Homo economicus*. But unpaid work done in the home indirectly enables a great deal of other productivity. Unpaid work in the home functions a bit like a natural resource that seems free – like clean water, fresh air. It is all around us and so obvious that we don't even notice it. It flies under the radar, completely invisible on the economic map. Not even a flashing dot. So it is not part of the economic system.

Many countries, particularly in the Western world, have responded by trying to transform unpaid domestic work into paid employment. That's one way of doing it. Some countries have created a comprehensive childcare system, which enables all parents, women and men, to work. Most people who work in childcare are – you guessed it – women. They get paid, but not a lot. So that's a step along the way, but maybe not the perfect solution.

Similar developments have occurred in other types of care, such as looking after elderly and long-term sick people. That work is now on the economic radar.

It is not entirely clear what this means for productivity in an economy. We can define productivity as how much we produce per hour worked, but that only counts hours worked for pay. If a worker's performance on the job requires them to turn up fed, happy, with a freshly ironed shirt and confident that someone at home is looking after the children, that means an invisible factor – another person – is contributing to their productivity. How do we measure that? The answer is that we probably don't.

Unpaid domestic labour could be seen as an invisible *external resource*. Care is also a mutually emotional, social relationship. I look after you, or you look after me. It makes us happy. That's not recorded in economic statistics either, as long as no one is paying. But perhaps it should be recorded somehow, if the whole idea of economic activity is to achieve greater prosperity.

The common image of economic activity as competition between individuals is a metaphor, a comparison we use to help us understand what's going on. But the comparison can be misleading. We like to think that it's how things happen in nature: that the struggle between various species of animals and plants drives change. But that's not really how it happens, at least not in the natural world – which we humans are a part of. Maybe we're misled by the idea that a species is an individual, and another species is another individual. But nature is more of a competition in cooperation.

Charles Darwin is often associated with the phrase 'survival of the fittest.' But he was not the one who came up with it. The phrase was first coined by Herbert Spencer, a 19th-century British economist. Darwin then simply borrowed the phrase and used it as an alternative to his own concept of *natural selection*, in later editions of his book *On the Origin of Species*.

Herbert Spencer was the editor of *The Economist*, a weekly magazine that is still in existence. In addition to being an eminent economist, Spencer was also a philosopher, biologist, anthropologist and sociologist. He published his own theory of evolution two years before Darwin's book came out. In his theory, Spencer compared society to a biological organism that evolves into higher, more complex forms through natural selection. While Spencer advocated public welfare to help society's poorest and most vulnerable, many of his contemporaries were less generous. For example, Francis Galton, a cousin of Charles Darwin, was one of the least altruistic. He believed that psychiatric hospitals and handouts for the poor just made social problems worse, because they let inferior, low-status individuals reproduce and increase in number.

Later, such extreme ideas in favour of unfettered competition, and the belief that rich people achieved their wealth by being better and stronger than others, were called *social Darwinism*. That's relevant for us in this book because this bundle of theories and opinions matches the unfavourable view of capitalism and economics in their most ruthless form. The term 'social Darwinism' appeared in the 1870s, but was only used by a few people. It was applied mainly to the sort of brutal commercial competition and the view of humans that was prevalent in the USA, and to some extent in Europe, in the late 19th and early 20th centuries. That era was known as the *Gilded Age* in America. Note that it was not called the *Golden Age*. 'Gilded' refers to something that is not solid gold, just a thin layer on the surface.

At that time, trading was simply seen as a brutal competition, just like in the natural world. This was the era of dodgy fictional characters like Ebenezer Scrooge: men in top hats, with bushy sideburns, who quickly amassed vast fortunes. They competed to build skyscrapers, each taller than the last. Twenty storeys, 50 storeys, 100 storeys! The tallest building in the world! In the basement, they had bank vaults filled with gold coins and fat bundles of cash. Beggars sat on the pavement in front. They were matched by real-life railway barons and monopolists like Cornelius Vanderbilt, Andrew Carnegie and many more.

In the spirit of that time, many of those men maintained that the poor should be self-reliant, with no outside help. People needed to be shaped in battle and competition with one another, and the strongest and healthiest would win. And if you won, that proved you were the most deserving. Politics and economics, both influenced by free interpretations of Darwin, were intertwined.

People who view society as consisting of individuals are called *individualists*. Individuals are also central to liberalism, which emphasises individual freedom. Everyone is unique; every person has their own human rights. When this liberal outlook is combined with elements of the theory of evolution, we end up with what is called *laissez-faire capitalism*. *Laissez-faire* is French for 'let them do' or 'let them go.' It is an old expression coined by François Quesnay (1694–1774), a French physician and economist. In his era, the term 'economist' was brand new. His ideas lived on among British liberal thinkers. The message was essentially to let people do as they pleased, since they knew best. The state should not get involved, because it would only make things worse. Individuals should compete instead, and then things would turn out well. This economic approach would re-emerge in Western countries around a century later, in the 1970s and 1980s, when it was called *neoliberalism*.

Today, we know that it doesn't work to draw social or economic conclusions from Darwin's theory of evolution the way the social Darwinists theorised. They are just free interpretations and analogies. Comparisons can help to explain things. But they can also confuse matters.

Sometimes the *invisible hand* can poke us in the eye. It needs rules to do its job well. Actually, it's simpler than that. It needs stable conditions so that we are able and willing to exchange things with one another. We have to be able to trust that the person we are trading with is not out to trick us. If I give you two sacks of barley and a sack of hops, and ask for a barrel of beer in exchange, I need to know the barrel is the size we agreed and you haven't diluted the beer with water. And you, in turn, have to be able to trust me.

Even the ancient bookkeeper Kushim's kinsfolk in the towns of Mesopotamia and Babylonia understood this principle. King Hammurabi issued laws that decreed how and when loans were to be repaid, and how written contracts should be made. Anyone intending to deposit gold or silver at the bank should first visit a notary and obtain a written record of the quantity of precious metals in their possession. Everything should be done by the book, so that no one got cheated.

If you do business with people in other cities or in faraway countries, you have to be certain you will receive the goods you order for the price you agree to pay. First of all, you and your colleagues need to know that all the merchants and salespeople involved in the deal are reliable, the quality is good and the price will not change. Then, there is a risk that unforeseen events could affect your deal. Highway robbers might come along and steal the cargo of spices and fabrics; a new government might introduce tariffs; an epidemic might suddenly halt all forms of transport. Any of these things could happen, even when things have been running smoothly for decades.

Settlements called *caravanserais* sprang up along the Silk Road, the celebrated trade route across Asia. They were small inns where camel caravans could stay and rest. Equally important for trade between China and the West was the Chinese emperor's establishment of regulations and a support organisation for merchants along the Silk Road. Ibn Battuta, a legendary 14th-century Arab explorer, described the system: each Chinese inn had an official who came with his secretary every evening to note down the names of travellers staying there. Then the doors were locked. The following morning, the names were recorded again after a roll call. One of the officials was tasked with accompanying the travellers to the next stopping point and returning with confirmation that all of the commercial travellers had arrived safely. Each inn had everything travellers needed in terms of overnight accommodation and food, particularly ducks and geese, as Ibn Battuta noted, though he was disappointed at the lack of sheep.

Nowadays, we also have trade agreements. Business news reports are often peppered with references to them in the form of acronyms or abbreviations. After the Second World War, the Western world introduced the General Agreement on Tariffs and Trade (GATT), the World Trade Organization (WTO) and the International Monetary Fund (IMF). And of course there's the Europen Union (EU). All of these organisations are pros at optimising conditions for trading things and writing rules to make trading as smooth and fair as possible. We might like to poke fun at the EU's attempts to define sizes of carrots to the nearest millimetre, but they do it in order to minimise the risk of buyers, sellers and consumers of carrots being deceived. Clearly, there is still room for improvement in the rules.

There are other reasons to regulate the economy besides national and international trade. If you want to borrow money, you have to provide some sort of security to the bank and demonstrate that you have a regular income. You need documents to prove you own a piece of land, a house or an apartment that can serve as collateral for your loan. You also need evidence of your salary, such as an employment contract or pay slips. These agreements and contracts only work in a society that has laws and rules – the framework that's necessary for the free market's actors and acrobats to move freely. They are the boundaries in which the players can improvise.

It is a mistake to think that a market economy always functions better with *fewer* rules. If you remove all these rules and laws, you will end up with anarchy, an informal economy, the sort of conditions that prevail in slum districts around the world. People in these places work hard, but they live in very insecure conditions and relative poverty. It is hard for them to build up long-term prosperity.

Instead, the economy works better if you have *good* rules. Not too many, but not too few either. It's not just the quantity but the *quality* of the rules that matters – what they regulate, and the amount of time and energy the market participants have to devote to following them. If the system is bureaucratic and time-consuming, it will stifle a lot of economic activity. It will also stifle innovation and initiative.

You can also imagine an economy with lots of rules, but the rules are easy to follow and each rule makes it easier for you to do business. The content of the laws and rules are the most important thing. If they are formulated sensibly, prevent actions that are harmful to society and reward actions that are beneficial to society, then a market economy – including all the people in that society who act out of their economic interests – will see positive development. We end up with a functioning market that benefits from many people's initiative, flexibility, innovation and cooperation. Therefore, laws and rules are not opposed to a *free* market economy, they are a part of it, just as laws and equality before the law, voting rights and freedom of expression are part of a free society, a *free* democracy.

The Peruvian economist Hernando de Soto has attracted attention for his idea that many people in developing countries could be helped by an information framework that records their ownership of property. They might live in a simple shack they built themselves, but they have no proof that they own either their home or the land it sits on. That means they are unable to borrow money secured on their house or land. Cities in Latin America, Africa and Asia have large informal districts, built without planning permission, on land with unclear ownership. In Brazil, these districts are known as *favelas*, a type of slum. De Soto says that the large informal sector of these countries' economies makes it difficult for people to lift themselves out of poverty, despite their hard work and inventiveness. They work in a shadow economy.

Only when the right sorts of laws and rules are in place can the invisible hand have free rein.

Strange, isn't it?

CAPITAL

In which we examine
what capital is, find out how
technology can involve cooperation
and take part in the launch
of a stock market.

OLD KARL WAS RIGHT.
Karl Marx, that is.

He wanted workers to own the essential tools for creating value. Today, we – the people of the world – possess the most crucial asset of all: creativity. Ultimately, our brains create our wealth. Maybe things have always been that way. But, at this particular place and time in our history, at the start of the 21st century, we can clearly see that our ideas and our intellect are our most important resource – our unique capital. Everything else, we can buy! It's the same for everyone. Nobody stands out with Microsoft software, a Huawei network or Siemens air conditioning. You, me and our seven billion or so brothers and sisters bring the uniqueness.

We live on a spherical marketplace that zooms through space. In a brief span of time, we have transformed our planet into a single huge bazaar. We trade with one another. We talk to one another. We play with one another. We set up markets for everything, everywhere – a spider's web of commerce and connections that spans our globe. And never have so many humans been able to live such long, fairly tolerable lives. Yes, Karl Marx was right, but he was also wrong. Communism is nearly extinct. Out of the 200 or so countries in the world, only North Korea is treading its own path, practising a homespun blend of communism and religion. The rest of us trade with one another in various marketplaces. In ordinary terms, it's what we call the market economy. In more formal – or more hateful – contexts, we call it capitalism.

Capital. Capitalists. Capitalism. Savour those words. They are strong words, emotionally charged.

Capital is a fuzzy word. Big and clear, yet also hard to pin down. Like a cloud, perhaps. From a distance, its contours are distinct, but, as you get closer, the edges become blurred.

Nevertheless, there are ways to explain what capital is and what it is not.

Long ago, the noisy, unruly bunch that is the world's economists designated 'capital' as one of four resources needed to produce a good or service. The other three are land, labour and organisation of labour. In the economists' view, capital encompasses various types of equipment, such as machines and tools that can come in handy when you want to produce something. Think of a traditional, old-fashioned factory, full of mysterious machines and other specialised equipment needed in the manufacturing process. In this context, 'capital' means things that have a physical presence: they are in the factory, and you can touch them. Besides their use in production, they also have monetary value. Sometimes a lot. Sometimes a little. At any rate, that's the definition economists use. When non-economists think about capital, it's usually that made-up stuff called money we think of. Both approaches make sense. As we have seen, money can be converted into buildings, machines or other things.

Whichever definition we choose, we can say that capital is something created by people. It does not occur in nature. You don't just find capital lying around the place. In the beginning, there was no capital. If you read the Bible or another holy book, it is clear that the beginning of the world was entirely free from capital. So, if there was no capital to start with, it must have come about as the result of something. That magical *something* is our inventiveness. It's what makes all the things we call innovations and inventions possible. All the wealth we have created, the long lives many of us will lead and all the prosperity we have achieved are simply the consequences of our desire and ability to invent unexpected things.

So, the demand for what has come to be called capital, and the existence of capital itself, is the result of thousands of years of making things: buildings, factories, machines. 'Capital' and 'capitalism' don't actually refer to the driving force behind our economic system. They're more about something that is a (by)product of our economic system. Deirdre McCloskey, an American professor of economics and history, has proposed the term *innovism* to refer to our powers of innovation, which are at the heart of the whole system.

Few things in our society have been the subject of as much brainwork and argument as the system known as capitalism. There has been no shortage of analysis and debate. Sometimes, the issue of whether capitalism should be allowed to exist at all has been taken to an extreme, resulting in war. We have tried to understand it. Sometimes, we have upended the whole thing. Everyone has been involved: intellectuals and politicians; guerilla commanders side by side with pop stars and the odd poet. For and against.

Perhaps the very topic is provocative – the idea that a little concept should determine the framework for essentially all human activity, like an immersive videogame we've all been born inside. It's actually very difficult to try to live *outside* some form of capitalism. Sometimes, it is nearly impossible to talk about economics without also talking about politics, directly or indirectly. The way things are gets mixed up with the way things ought to be. Beliefs get mixed up with facts. But we'll put our high horses out to pasture, here. They're likely to rear up.

Instead, let's travel back in time. In this book, you will learn that there are three evolutions, revolutions or discoveries that have shaped our economic system. The first was the simple yet powerful realisation that a few simple actions can make everyone better off. It's our apes and their exchange, in its most basic form. As we have seen, the nice thing about exchanging things is that both parties often end up better off. Exchanging is another way of describing people's division of labour – the practice that so impressed Adam Smith in the pin factory. Initially, bartering involved a very simple division of labour. You're good at picking nuts; I'm good at picking figs. I know of a nice stand of fig trees. I'm quick and have picked lots of figs. Let's trade. It was simple and easy to grasp for everyone involved.

Over time, the division of labour became more advanced. Even before we started farming and living in cities, we discovered the power of becoming a specialist. Hunter-gatherer societies employ the division of labour in many ways. Their very name contains one example: hunters and gatherers. Some people hunt, others gather. One person might be good at gathering nuts, while others are good at gathering medicinal plants. One person is good at hunting birds; someone else is good at hunting deer. Someone is good at making bows and arrows; someone else is good at making flint axes. Let's trade.

In the second evolution, we discovered that, the more people get involved and exchange things, the better our chances of finding the things we want. Exchanging has an interest in spreading, like a virus (only it spreads happiness, rather than sickness and death). The more people who join the party, the better. We can either travel further to find more people to exchange with, or we can find better ways of communicating with the people nearby. Better transport and better communications make it easier to cooperate and specialise.

In the third evolution, we invented what we call *money*. Instead of carrying nuts, fruit or animal pelts around, we came up with an invented item that everyone wanted, which was easy to store and transport. When everyone wanted that made-up item – in our era, it could be US dollars – we had taken the third and perhaps most remarkable step towards what would later be called a *global economy*. We had developed a sort of universal system that enabled total strangers, without even a shared language, to exchange things with one another. If you want to be dramatic, you could say that it was the final step in building the magical mechanism that can transform a farmer's apples into a fish. A cobbler's shoes can be transformed into a horse and a bottle of wine. And a fortune teller can transform predictions about her clients' future into food, shelter and a cradle. Money makes exchanging things much more efficient. Everyone can use it in transactions with everyone else.

As we have seen, trading today has few to no limits. Specialisation has increased, and we produce more and more things. So many, in fact, that we are starting to think they constitute a problem in our part of the world. Our wealth is overflowing. There are things everywhere. We don't have space in our homes for all the things. We watch YouTube videos about strong-willed people who make their homes into oases of calm, freed from unnecessary possessions. We hire consultants to help us declutter our homes. Our possessions become rubbish, and then rubbish mountains. Even so, they are amazing, the things we've made. Capital.

Technology could be regarded as formalised human cooperation. Our possessions are human cooperation that has taken on physical form. A simple pencil we use for writing is the result of sophisticated cooperation among many people. We trade to obtain it and then write a book. A bottle of wine is also the result of cooperation among many people: vintners, grape pickers, bottle manufacturers. Many hours of coordinated labour is contained in a single bottle.

This is where we might find the roots of capitalism. Labour specialisation and cooperation are the explanation for the vast growth capitalism has brought about. Industrialisation and the market economy have boosted our standard of living to unprecedented levels; average life expectancy has increased and health care has improved, along with housing and much more. But technology and material goods, like so many other things, have a good side and a bad side. They spurred growth, but they are also the source of the sustainability issues we see in so many areas today.

Capitalism can be defined in many ways. One definition is based on ownership. It says that capitalism is an economic system in which the means of production – things that are needed to manufacture goods – are owned by private individuals – either separately, or as shareholders in companies. All goods and services are then bought and sold in the open market. This definition also fits the term *market economy*, which is the opposite of a pure *planned economy*, in which all the means of production are owned by the state, and only indirectly by the people. Goods and services that are produced within the planned economy are then distributed based on a plan that is highly complex and difficult to administer – unworkable, actually, as the attempts in the Soviet Union and other communist countries showed. Those attempts were also combined with authoritarian, undemocratic governments that suppressed freedom of expression.

But the specific origin of the word *capitalism* lies in a peculiar feature of one sort of market economy that rose to prominence during the Industrial Revolution. That peculiarity was that the wealth, or capital, that merchants amassed through their sales and trading was not spent on extravagant mansions and parties. Instead, those businessmen ploughed a great deal of their profits back into their businesses. They *invested* in machines, buildings and other capital to make their businesses more efficient. Perhaps a brand-new machine could increase efficiency at a sewing-pin factory, or building another factory could double production capacity. In other words, capital could make production more efficient and therefore more profitable. The first million is the hardest.

Once you've got a bit of money – a bit of capital – to invest, it's easier to acquire more capital – assuming you invest it well, of course. Capital is simply a *tool* to earn more money, which then enables you to invest in even more capital. This is an inherent property of capitalism. In the first century of industrialisation, capital was primarily invested in *things*: machines, buildings, vehicles. Then capital became more intangible. Over time, investments in licensing, patents, know-how and other intellectual property – that is, the sort of things you can't drop on your foot – took on as much or more importance than physical assets, especially for businesses.

As we have already seen, technology and machines are expressions of a form of division of labour: specialisation with built-in leverage. Think about the old-fashioned concept of *horsepower*. It is usually defined as the amount of work a horse can perform during one day of continuous work. But how much is that? Someone calculated that one horsepower is equivalent to lifting a 75 kg (165 lb) weight one metre (39 inches) up in the air for one second. That's pretty heavy. Another way of expressing it is to say that one horsepower is equivalent to a person who weighs 75 kg going up six stairs (one metre in height difference) in one second. That's also hard work, so we should regard machines as our friends.

Machines can help us do things we would never manage otherwise. Not in a reasonable amount of time, anyway. A car's engine has a certain number of horsepower. If you can afford a horse, that's good, because you will reach your destination quicker than you would without it, and you can carry a heavier load. A horse is ten times stronger than a person. But, if you can afford a 50-horsepower engine, you are now 50 times stronger than a horse. A small car for city driving will often have an engine that produces 75 to 100 horsepower. It doesn't need many breaks, and it rarely gets tired. It's a fantastic, efficient machine when we need to get a certain type of work done. That's physics. And that's capitalism. Its material aspects are interrelated with money. No money, no machine.

If you want to be able to afford machines, you might need to borrow money from the bank. Or you could get other people to invest in the machine required to carry out your idea. There you are, with your idea, and you need a million kronor to make it happen. You could find a millionaire and persuade them to invest, or you could find 1,000 people who are willing to invest 1,000 kronor each. The choice is yours. But this is where it starts to get risky. Not all ideas become successful.

Some people have a negative view of capitalism. They associate it with taking risks, gambling and inequality. But it can also possess an incredible allure. That's because it encompasses a system that makes us wealthier year on year. It rewards us and advances our society, extends our lives and lessens inconveniences. As a system, it is far superior to a dysfunctional planned economy. But capitalism can also have something to do with speculation – with money that is easy come, easy go. In a capitalist system, some people may even lose their savings. All of these associations contain a grain of truth, as we shall see.

Capitalism, capital, the stock market and risk are all connected. And the stock market is connected to business travel: our seafaring friends who went out in search of spices and other tasty things; a gamble that started in Amsterdam, and still affects your personal finances today – to a great degree, and more than you realise.

The Dutch lagged a bit behind the Portuguese, Arabs, Chinese and Spanish in terms of trading, as we have seen in earlier chapters, but they were keen to get involved in lucrative trade expeditions. They were particularly interested in acquiring spices from India. In the late 16th century, the various regions of the Netherlands finally united to form a federal republic – a huge achievement in Europe at that time, which was an unruly patchwork of absolute monarchies. Amsterdam was particularly fertile ground for people who had good ideas or were fleeing persecution. It offered a relatively good level of religious freedom. In an earlier chapter, we met the cosmopolitan Johan Palmstruch in Amsterdam. He was the slightly shady inventor of paper banknotes. Like so many others, he was drawn to Amsterdam during an economic boom triggered by the spice trade and the financial innovations that accompanied it. People from all parts of Europe made their way to Amsterdam, including many Jews who had been expelled from Portugal and Spain. The newcomers brought knowledge with them. Rumours circulated of a faraway island called Java that was bursting with spices, which the Portuguese had not yet reached.

The first voyage to Java nearly ended in disaster, much as it had done for Vasco da Gama. After two years at sea, three of the expedition's four vessels returned, with just 89 of their original 249 crewmen. The voyage did make a profit, in purely financial terms. The merchants who had invested in the voyage liquidated the company and shared the profits between themselves. That's how they did things, back then. When the voyage was complete, the company would be dissolved, like a disposable business. The endeavour was finished, so the company was no longer needed. Very handy. Within a few years, another 65 Dutch vessels set sail for Java and the Spice Islands. They made big profits. Then the European market was awash with pepper, so the price there declined. Meanwhile, believing there was a high demand, having sold so much pepper, the sellers in Indonesia raised their prices.

When profitability took a hit and competition got tougher, the Dutch decided to combine their trade voyages into a single company, which they named the Dutch East India Company, or Verenigde Oost-Indische Compagnie (abbreviated VOC). This was followed by one economic innovation after another. You could say that it marked the birth of a new form of capitalism.

The first major decision was to make VOC a permanent business, not another disposable company. It would not be dissolved at the end of a voyage. Another key decision was that, after all the shares in the company had been purchased, they could be sold on – under certain conditions, of course. By the book. If you wanted to sell your shareholding in VOC, you had to visit the head office together with the buyer and have the transaction registered. You paid a small sum to the bookkeeper and a tax. The second-hand market in company shares was up and running.

Trade voyages to the East Indies took a long time, anywhere between 15 months and several years. While a voyage was underway, reports would come in of storms, wars, epidemics or good trading and bumper cargoes. Expectations of profits, whether large or small, waxed and waned. People would gather on a bridge over the Damrak (part of the Amstel River), not far from VOC's head office, to buy and sell shares in the company.

That was the start of the stock market. Most of the people who invested were already well off, but the system of share ownership meant that even craftsmen and other citizens of the Dutch Republic could invest – and earn – money in the East Indies spice trade.

The value of shares could go up a little or a lot. Or they could crash. Some people grew fabulously wealthy. Others did not. How could they deal with that uncertainty?

The basic idea of a share is very simple. It means you own part, or a share, of a company. As a share owner, you are entitled to part of the company's profit, which is known as a *dividend*. Dividends are often given out at the end of each year. If you lived in 17th-century Amsterdam, you would have waited for a ship or ships to return from Java; the VOC's shippers would then sell their cargo of pepper and count up the profit. You would get your portion.

But maybe you needed your money during the year, in which case you could sell your share. Or, if you doubted the ships would make it through the autumn gales to reach home port, but you happened to meet an incurable optimist who had heard there were no storms that year, you could agree on a price higher than you thought your share would be worth at the end of the year. That way, you avoid the risk of losing your money. The pessimist sells. The optimist buys and assumes the risk, but also gets the chance of a profit if all the ships make it back.

Soon enough, the next innovation came along: options. An option is the *right* to buy or sell shares for a fixed price in the *future*. An option takes on a value of its own. It is not a share of ownership; it is merely the right to buy or sell a share at a particular price in the future. The dizzying financial aspect of the economy had started to emerge. Over time, it became clear that the only limit on how far things could go was the imagination – or, in some cases, the law.

The title of this chapter is *Capital*, which is also the title of a well-known book by Karl Marx, who has already been mentioned. A sort of sequel to that book was published several years ago, entitled *Capital in the Twenty-First Century*, by Thomas Piketty, a French economist. Piketty sets out a lengthy historical analysis of economic inequality in the

Western world. How is capital distributed, and why? Basically, he concludes that, in our economy, people earn more money by owning things than by working. In economists' language, returns on capital – owning – accumulate faster than economic growth. In more everyday language, that means you can earn more by owning money and other assets than by doing anything else. Piketty says that one part of the economic pie – namely, various types of capital – has started to grow more rapidly than the rest of the pie.

In an ordinary year, household wealth, or the things you or I own, should grow at roughly the same rate as the economy as a whole. However, things have not worked that way for a long time. If the monetary supply increases for some reason, such as through bank lending or government stimulus programmes, wealth in the form of shares or real estate can continue growing faster than the rest of the economy. Household wealth can even grow when the economy shrinks. That's what happened during the pandemic. Hard-hit countries, such as Belgium, the UK, Canada and Singapore, saw their economies *shrink*, but huge economic support packages caused wealth to *grow*.

Piketty's hypothesis is that, over time, wealth represents an ever-greater share of the economy, creating huge inequalities. If capital consistently grows faster than the rest of the economy, year after year, then the economy will become increasingly concentrated among the owners of capital. Many people have debated the accuracy of Piketty's theory and the measures that should be taken if his theory is accurate. There is no doubt that Piketty has helped to make it clear that looking at wage income alone is insufficient to understand a society. You also need to consider wealth and returns on capital. There's that word *capital* again.

While Piketty, the French economist, is looking at the issue from a left-leaning perspective, the Swiss bank Credit Suisse views things in a different light in its Global Wealth Report, which is published every year. The Swiss bankers' publication, which focuses on wealth, both confirms what Piketty says and gives a more detailed analysis. Credit Suisse agrees that wealth has become increasingly concentrated among the richest segment – particularly the very richest 1% – but that doesn't necessarily mean the wealth has been stolen from the poorest. Rather, the amount of capital has increased, as we have seen. The economy is not a zero-sum game, where one person's gain is automatically another's loss – we learned that in the first chapter. To summarise: a great many people are better off now, but the rich have become richer even faster. One per cent now owns nearly half.

The role of financial capital in capitalism is to invest in productive assets – machinery, factories, distribution and so on – to raise productivity and create jobs. The idea behind Reaganomics, the 1980s brand of neoliberalism in the US, was that, by reducing tax on capital gains and high earners' incomes, wealthy people would retain more money, which they could invest. In theory, that would lead to higher productivity, more new businesses and ultimately higher economic growth that would benefit everyone. But it didn't seem to work, at least not in the US. The intended impact was not noticeable. In fact, things moved in the opposite direction. Taxes on high incomes, marginal tax brackets and capital gains were halved between 1990 and 2020. But the wealth held by the top half of the population increased, while economic growth slowed. Growth in the US for the period from 1990 to 2020 was just half that from 1950 to 1990. In Sweden and other Western countries, we have more billionaires than ever, but our productivity is stagnant. One could argue that the decrease in growth is due to reasons other than reductions in income tax and capital-gains tax – that is, tax rates on those items do not influence growth. But that also defeats the argument for cutting those taxes to spur economic growth, job creation, productivity and innovation.

Nowadays, the most common way to make really big money is not by having a high salary, but by owning some sort of asset – owning a house or other real estate. Or by owning shares or other financial instruments. At some point, we need to address the elephant in the room: our mortgages. Mortgages have made a very large number of people who own their homes, especially in the Western world, into capitalists – whether they realise it or not. The elephant just keeps growing. It got a big boost from more than ten years' worth of low interest rates after the 2007–8 financial crisis. In the last couple of decades, a Swedish homeowner would have made thousands of kronor a month on their home as property prices rose. If you owned a house or apartment in a booming housing market, somewhere like Stockholm, in recent years, you might have made as much as 20,000 kronor a month, purely in terms of increasing property values, as a result of starting out with a bit of capital which you could borrow money on and grow. But you wouldn't have produced anything. Of course, you'd have a place to live, but overall productivity in society didn't increase. That's assuming we don't think that rising prices for housing in popular city-centre locations *are* good for productivity in society.

We can see similar trends all over the world. Capital is growing faster than the rest of the economy. There are many ways of calculating this, but the pattern has continued throughout the post-Second World War era, and the tendency has accelerated in the last 40 years. Since 1980, the global economy has expanded sevenfold. The total value of international trade is ten times what it was. But financial capital has increased by a factor of between 25 and 35.

The lion's share of that capital has been used to purchase real estate – mainly homes, but also commercial properties. That's why home prices have increased. As we saw in chapter two, about money and banking, banks can create new money by granting loans – then, the amount of capital increases. Although some capital goes towards the purchase of brand-new homes, mostly it goes towards purchasing existing ones.

The figures for Sweden display the same pattern. The total money supply, or capital, is increasing far faster than the number of homes. The number of homes in Sweden grew by just 25% between 1990 and 2020. The monetary supply – that is, the total amount of money in society – increased by a factor of seven in the same period, according to Statistics Sweden. So that's seven times more money chasing an almost unchanged number of homes.

It's no surprise, then, that house prices have gone up. In Sweden, prices have increased by 7% annually for the last 30 years. That might not sound like much, but a 7% increase every year means that the value doubles in ten years. Over a decade, one million becomes two million. After another ten years, that two million becomes four. And, yes, after 30 years it becomes eight million. No wonder interest is sometimes called the eighth wonder of the world.

Meanwhile, capital that's used for productive investments, the linchpin of capitalism – remember the machines in the pin factory – that portion of capital is still at the same level as in 1980. The only country that has actually increased its investment in machinery and other productive assets is China. They have built a lot of new infrastructure, including the new Silk Road, to increase their nation's influence and stimulate its growth. That matters in the global economy. In Sweden, the situation resembles that in other Western countries. Here, nearly 90% of money is spent on financial investments like shares and – that's right – homes and real estate. Just over 10% goes into other investments. One krona in ten.

What can we do with all this information? A great many people are better off. Even so, it feels strange on an intuitive level that the wealthiest 1% will soon own half of everything. It feels unfair. Or maybe that's a good thing? Can the quantity of capital continue to grow indefinitely, in comparison to the real economy? How great the disparities in a society can be, or should be, is an ethical matter – and, by extension, a political matter.

What kind of society do we want? This sort of question is difficult, if not impossible, to answer via research. Science can't always help us decide what's important or how we should apply some particular knowledge. Perhaps moral philosophy is what's called for, here – Adam Smith's specialist subject. What is good? What is morally right? Those are questions we can discuss, debate and philosophise about. From a strictly scientific perspective, it is unclear what we should do with more knowledge about topics like economic disparity. Should we use that knowledge to try to increase wealth accumulation for a few people and hope it will benefit everyone in the long run? Or should we let the state take over and even out incomes as well as wealth? Obviously, communist, fascist and liberal governments and policymakers would reach different conclusions – and make different choices based on the same information, the same numbers.

That's exactly what happens in the real world. Countries, governments and regions make their own ideological choices. Even though all the countries in the world are market economies – with the exception of the aforementioned North Korea, still going against the grain – the nature of those market economies can differ greatly. The USA and the Nordic countries are all market economies, but they have differing views of what should be controlled and how. Denmark believes in high taxes on salaries, while the US taxes them at a lower rate. While Sweden does not tax certain things at all – such as estates that are inherited – the American position is that large estates are taxed quite heavily.

If capitalism were a language, we might say that everyone now speaks it, but with different dialects.

What we refer to as *capital* is growing.

And the economy is changing its nature.

It is becoming increasingly financial.

And fuzzier.

Financial instruments are becoming more abstract. They are based on, and extract value from, the tangible type of capital that increases productivity in a business – a sort of lever on top of another lever.

Ordinary capital, if we can call it that, in turn bases its value creation on various types of natural resources and energy introduced into the system.

But that's not visible.

Nature is very far away from the world of digital finance.

We are here, in the ultra-modern, interconnected, 21st-century Anthropocene world. Video games are by far our greatest commercial expression of culture. Money is now zeros and ones. Made-up private currencies, like bitcoin and ether, are starting to challenge nation states' traditional monetary systems. Like termites, cryptocurrencies are making many inroads in the financial structure. Sustainability is becoming a necessary but not sufficient criterion for any transaction in many parts of the world.

And the question everyone is asking is whether our ceaseless trading is the problem or the solution to the major problems of our era.

THE EARTH AND GROWTH

In which we build megacities, let our cows graze outdoors, and enjoy coffee, cake and doughnuts.

That's how we think about it – in images.

We want things to *grow*, branch out. Companies should *flourish*, like in the natural world.

This metaphor seems to appeal to us primates. But then – maybe without even realising – we started to think that growth no longer had anything to do with nature.

We had entered version 2.0 – something completely different.

But, if we slow down and think about it, all economic activity is founded on nature. How could it be founded on anything else? All we started with were the resources in the Earth, water and air, energy from the Sun. Earth, Sun, air, water – a bit like the four elements.

This has not always been clear in economic thought in recent years. Or, more accurately, it wasn't something we thought about in great detail. And that's not so strange. People often say that economics is the study of scarce resources – a sort of fancy domestic science. But, if we don't realise that a resource is scarce – if it is extremely abundant – then we don't need to ration it. Fair enough – for a while, anyway. Nowadays, everybody understands that even a high-tech Silicon Valley start-up is part of nature's self-contained cycle. Engineers with bright ideas drink their soy lattes from Japanese jujube-wood mugs. Marvellous. But those trees have to grow somewhere.

We also like to dig. Alongside the renewable circle of life, we dig finite resources out of the ground through mining. Things like silicon for circuit boards, or lithium for car batteries. We drill for oil. Of course, oil and coal come from organisms that lived long ago. Everything comes from the Earth – we've just had a tendency to forget that. For a long time, there were few of us, and the planet was so, so big.

In 1800, nearly everyone was a farmer. That's only a bit more than 200 years ago. A ridiculously short period. Just 3% of the world's people lived in cities then. Most cities were relatively small – especially compared to 21st-century megacities. Once again, industrialisation drove this transformation.

Economists back then counted the land as a key resource – which was entirely reasonable in a world where the vast majority of people lived off the land. Land, labour, capital – those were the building blocks of the economy. Then, as industrialisation increased, that stuff about *land* went out of fashion. We progressed from an agrarian society to an industrial society. That's the narrative we were taught at school.

Then, at the end of the 19th century, things really ramped up. First in Britain, where women and men left the countryside and made their way to the cities and the new factories there. They found jobs on the assembly lines. They purchased their food at the local shop. It was not only a new home, but a whole new lifestyle. *Urbanisation* is the term used for mass migration into cities. The trend spread across Europe and then to North America. New York – which could be called the post-war global capital city – had a population of ten million in 1950, up from about three and a half million in 1900. The wave of urbanisation continued to Asia. At the start of the 21st century, seven of the world's ten largest cities are in Asia.

Another shift occurred in parallel with urbanisation – a shift in mindset. The United States, Canada and the nations of Europe had long been called *industrialised nations*, and they belonged to the *industrialised world*. After so many years of increasing prosperity, we simply referred to our part of the world in terms of what had made us rich: industry and factories. Other parts of the world were referred to as *developing countries*, as if they were following in our footsteps – the aspiring newbies. For a long time, that was the established order.

In the 1990s, though, talk centred more on skills and the *knowledge economy*. Intellectual capital. The important stuff is between people's ears. After two centuries, factories and industry started to lose their lustre. Physical materials came to be regarded as less essential. Our prosperity is no longer forged from steel, but from knowledge – thoughts, ideas – and a great deal of imagination. Our future and economic growth are to be found in air-conditioned office buildings, behind smoked-glass windows. The origin of the metaphor behind the word *growth* – the natural world – was forgotten long ago. Once we realised that talent is what makes capital dance, our optimism knew no limits.

The hub of this new knowledge economy is the much-hyped Silicon Valley. There – half an hour's drive from San Francisco – we can find many of the first and biggest stars of what is sometimes called the *new economy*. In January 2022, Apple became the first company in the world to reach a stock-market value of three trillion dollars. Talent really does make capital rock the joint.

The knowledge economy fed into several new industries and phenomena. Soon, nearly every man and woman had their own mobile phone, and Internet connections became as ubiquitous as electricity. But the new companies and technologies also seemed to hasten the transformation of our societies. In 2009, the United Nations noted in its State of the World's Cities report that 50% of the world's population lived in cities. More and more people were moving to cities. Often, women are the first to leave and venture into cities. The UN predicts that, in 2050, three quarters of the global population will live in cities. The term *megacities* is increasingly popular: the category includes cities with populations over ten million. Places like Lagos in Nigeria, or Shenzhen in China are growing at incredible rates. Since the turn of the millennium, megacities have mushroomed in Asia. In 1985, there were nine megacities in the world. By 2020, there were around 35, half of which were located in India or China. In some places around the world, huge cities are merging into mega-regions. These are areas stretching for hundreds of kilometres that are home to hundreds of millions of people. Today, the biggest mega-region is located around the former British Crown colony of Hong Kong, with over 120 million people.

What does this have to do with land? From our perspective in the bustling, bright, noisy city, the countryside seems very far away. We have left nature behind. We're urbanites now. We move about in ravines of glass and steel, in the urban jungle. Food is something we buy in a supermarket or a fast-food place. And never have we traded as many things with one another as we do now. Large numbers of people in a small space provide the best conditions for specialisation and trading.

Large numbers of people in one place don't just create opportunities, though. There are also problems. For example, if we look at some of our megacities, we can clearly see that air pollution increases. It is literally *visible*. London was the largest city in the world for a hundred years up to the First World War. Its population in 1900 was around five million. The famous London fog in the 19th and 20th centuries was mostly not fog, but smog from coal fires. Pollution was such an integral part of the world's first industrialised country that it became part of its national identity – like the London fog, or the black façade of the prime minister's official residence at 10 Downing Street. When the exterior was cleaned as part of a thorough renovation in the early 1960s, the brickwork was revealed to be yellow. Its black colour, widely publicised since the invention of photography, was the result of severe pollution. After cleaning, the decision was made to paint the exterior brickwork black to restore its familiar appearance.

Of course, London's residents are now pleased to be free from such high levels of smog, and people in New Delhi, Beijing and other megacities would probably welcome clean air too. Air pollution in those cities far exceeds safe levels and clearly constitutes a health hazard. Burning coal in the expansive phase of industrialisation created great prosperity, but it also caused harm – then, as now. There are clear parallels with Britain's history. You can see the pollution in the new megacities with the naked eye, and you can feel in your throat and lungs how hard it is to breathe. If you place a white plastic chair outdoors in Beijing, it doesn't take long before you have to wipe it clean.

Other effects on our surroundings are less visible. They are harder to identify at the time, which makes them harder to counteract. This brings us from the air back down to Earth. Early economic thinkers talked about three fundamental things needed to produce anything: land, labour and capital. Those writers were products of their own time, as we are of ours. Of course land is an important factor in an agricultural society. Land and workers were the key production factors right up until the Industrial Revolution. As the basis of economic activity, they were more important than capital. Then, as industrialisation took hold in the 19th century and throughout the 20th, land gradually receded from view in economic theory and thinking.

Now, though, land has come to the fore again, after a couple of centuries. This time, our primary focus is on planet Earth, not the earth in which we grow crops. You might say that our interest is more biological than financial. It's about the planet as our home, rather than as a tool, and it's about saving the planet we call home. But, if we dig a little deeper into the earth, it turns out that it's also about – you guessed it – the economy.

You can think of economics and economic thinking as a language. So *land* has one meaning in economics and another meaning in biology. Viewed through the lens of biology, land is made up of a combination of minerals in different proportions (rock, sand, clay) and organic matter in the form of fungi, microorganisms, worms and plant materials at various stages of decomposition. Plants can take root and grow in the earth. They in turn help increase soil fertility by interacting with fungi and microorganisms, and by losing leaves and other parts that can be broken down. If the microorganisms disappear, the fertile land will deterioriate into sand and gravel. That is what has happened in a desert – like in Babylonia, old Kushim's homeland, if you remember him.

But 'land' and 'earth' have several additional meanings in economics. They are more than just the soil we cultivate. They mean natural resources. You could even go so far as to say that *earth* also refers to air, water and plants. It also means non-renewable natural resources like minerals and fossil fuels. (Additional fossil fuels continue to be formed, but because the process takes millions of years, they are regarded as non-renewable from our human perspective).

So, when we are speaking Economics, *land* is a place that has an owner. It is divided up into properties, which may be privately or publicly owned, by a country or a smaller entity. A third sort of property is a *commons*, the roots of which stretch far back in time. One concept that often comes up in political discourse is known as the *tragedy of the commons*. It is related to land and the Earth in a number of ways. Economists, anthropologists and sociologists started devoting more attention to commons in the 1960s, perhaps because the concept is distinct from both the inflexible planned economy and the wild market economy, yet it touches on them both. The commons can also be viewed as being about sustainability – the commons is like nature.

The story goes like this: there is a commons – a meadow that is owned in common by the neighbouring farms. Each farmer can let his cows graze on the commons, free of charge. All the farmers can use the meadow for free. In the story, the meadow ends up being overgrazed and ruined because it belongs to everyone and therefore no one.

There are different ways to interpret that story. One interpretation is that a limited resource that is free and accessible will end up being over-exploited. It will be damaged, temporarily or permanently. This happens because the benefits are visible and private, but the costs are hidden. Moreover, the costs are borne by the collective. Every farmer is motivated by his self-interest to graze his own cows as much as he can – after all, it's free. There are no short-term costs for the individual. Unfortunately, this principle applies to more than just grazing.

Fishing in international waters could be another example. If all the world's fishermen go out and haul in as much as they can, eventually there will be no fish left. The conclusion is that shared natural resources will be overexploited if it is possible to do so for free. The same reasoning can be applied to pollution. This goes some way towards explaining the tragedy resulting from our long-term neglect of nature. As long as it's free, we keep polluting.

Solutions to the tragedy of the commons are available. The choice of solution will be influenced by views on societal structures – politics, in other words. One solution is simply to privatise common resources. Divide them up. That can work, but some natural resources probably should remain intact. Another solution is for the state to step in and regulate and/or tax their usage. Before you decide which solution you think is best, bear in mind that the whole story is made up. It's a hypothetical situation. We know from experience that it might not be improbable. Shared kitchens in student accommodation are a sort of tragedy of the commons in miniature. Everyone's responsibility becomes no one's responsibility. The fridge is full of food that's gone off. People don't do the washing up. Nobody wipes the table.

Elinor Ostrom, the first woman to be awarded the Nobel Prize in Economics, studied commons that actually worked. They do exist. Many have worked for centuries, without being overexploited. Things that work are just as interesting as things that don't work. Ostrom studied *why* some commons worked. In simple terms, it depends on the users of the commons organising some sort of community that draws up rules on how and when the commons may be used. You can think of it as a sort of club. If someone doesn't follow the rules, they are punished – kicked out of the club. Ostrom identified eight design principles that seemed to recur in successful systems. She also found that *local* groups seemed to be the best at managing local ecosystems; they can spot early warning signals that something is starting to go wrong and avert a major tragedy.

The terms *economy*, *economics* and *ecology* come from the same root: *oikos*, which is Greek for 'household.' Ecology is the study of nature's household, the ecosystem, while economics is the study of the relationship between people and resources – nature and culture, you could say. One goes on existing with or without us – that's nature. Culture – well, that's us and what we think up. What we do and don't do. As mentioned previously, we usually say that economics is the study of dealing with scarce resources. If everything was abundant, we wouldn't need to bother. Our resources wouldn't be scarce, and we wouldn't need to study them.

Economists exist. Biologists and ecologists exist. We know more than ever before about both nature and culture. That's the good news. The not-so-good news is that, up until recently, we have lacked knowledge of how our ecosystem relates to our economic system. Or rather, how they should interact to avoid harm to the ecosystem, and later to our human economic system. When we know how something works, it's so much easier to agree on what can or should be done.

Our planet's ecosystem will presumably mutate and continue to exist in one form or another. Sir David Attenborough, the British naturalist and legendary broadcaster, has drily observed that nature doesn't have a problem; it is we *humans* who have problems. The plants, organisms and conditions we need to survive could become scarce or disappear. The question is: should we adapt nature to our economic system, or would it be easier to change our economic system to accommodate the ecosystem?

It's ultimately a matter of perspective and of our view of nature. Perspectives on nature have shifted over the course of history. Nature has been viewed as a powerful adversary to be conquered, as well as a fragile place with a soul that must be revered and protected. It has been construed both as an endless source of natural resources we can exploit, and as an integral part of ourselves and vice versa. Nature has posed existential questions for which science has only been able to provide partial answers.

There seems to be a realisation that we cannot blithely carry on in the same manner as before – among most people, anyway. People have even taken up sustainability as a competitive issue. Countries and businesses have got involved. But not everyone is on board. Plenty of people around the world still doubt whether climate change and global warming are real and are caused by humans. The sceptics are now (slightly) in the minority, though. Scientists have managed to convince governments that action is needed to stop climate change now. So, we are starting to agree on the existence of the problem, and its magnitude. That leaves the issue of *what* to do, and how much. And how fast. You know – little things.

It has taken time to reach this point. Step by step, our notions of the links between economics and ecology have changed. That can happen. Major insights often occur at the interface between two or more fields of knowledge. Sometimes, we use the word *paradigm*. Basically, it refers to a coherent world view or system of interrelated theories. Information or facts that do not fit a paradigm are waved aside or explained away.

Eventually, though, the contradictions accumulate until they are so obvious that the existing theories need to be replaced. This is called a *paradigm shift*. Centuries ago, Galileo's observations and measurements of the Sun and planets made us change our model in which the Sun revolved around the Earth to one in which the Earth revolves around the Sun. Economic science has undergone several paradigm shifts over the years. Could a new one be on its way? In any event, economics has gradually changed its attitude to nature and the notion of sustainability.

An initial step was taken back in the 1960s and 1970s, when people started to realise that, in addition to supplying us with products, factories also, in many cases, polluted the environment. White-tailed eagle populations were threatened. Fish suffered mercury poisoning. Dead birds, and lakes and rivers that were unfit for swimming, raised alarm bells around the world.

A decade or so later, a number of crises and disasters led to the concept of *sustainable development*, which encompasses much more than simply not polluting the environment. The term was coined in 1981 by Lester Brown, an American environmentalist. That was when the scientific community started to take a serious interest in the issue. It's worth noting that, at this point, women start to emerge as prominent names in our history of economics. Prior to this, their role in economics was significant, but anonymous. Now, we see names emerge like Elinor Ostrom, the Nobel laureate mentioned earlier, and Gro Harlem Brundtland, Norway's first female prime minister and later director-general of the World Health Organization. Brundtland is known for popularising a definition of sustainable development that is still in use, though today we tend to use the shorter term *sustainability*: 'Sustainable development is development that meets the needs of the present without compromising the ability of future generations to meet their own needs.'

Nature now had a place in the economy, covered by the 20th-century term *the environment*. It was generally accepted that, as long as polluting the environment carried no cost, it would continue. This is an example of what economists call an *externality*, or something that is outside or external. The term refers to a cost or benefit that affects someone who did not choose to receive it. The effect is indirect, caused by someone else's action. Externalities are everywhere. They are a fundamental principle. A farmer might let his cows graze on the commons all week; all the grass is gone; this angers the other farmers. You race your sports car through the city streets; other people are terrified and nearly get run over; what's more, your V8 engine pollutes the air they breathe, and your tyres shed toxic rubber particulates when you skid round corners.

If we think about it, most of what we do impacts our surroundings in one way or another. As usual, the simple principle applies: we don't care, as long as it's free. So we need to put a price on the negative effects of our economic growth. It has to take account of everything we do and don't do. The system we used to have, and to some extent still do, has led us astray. Destroying our environment is a hidden cost that we all share; those who exploit our resources avoid paying for it and so increase their profit margin, and the consumers of goods and services get all the joy. Our fellow human beings end up less joyful in the long run.

The idea of putting a price on emissions has led to a CO_2 tax in Sweden, for example – one of the first in the world. The more carbon emissions, the higher the tax and the more expensive the product. The intention is to use pricing to steer companies towards 'greener' production, and to steer us consumers towards greener consumption. If petrol is more expensive, we'll drive less. We are starting to put into practice the simple yet powerful idea that, as soon as something costs money, we care.

Another system that has emerged from the same simple idea is the EU emissions-trading system. In theory, this is how it works: the EU and its member states allocate rights to emit a certain limited quantity of carbon dioxide into the atmosphere. Like a sort of letter of environmental indulgence. Forgiveness for the sin of pollution, but only up to a point. The same rules apply to all businesses, according to a formula. The idea is that companies with clean production methods won't need to use their full quota of carbon credits and will have a surplus. Dirty, inefficient companies will have a hard time sticking to their quota. In order to keep producing, the inefficient companies will have to purchase carbon credits from the efficient factories. Over time, it will be expensive. The system aims to incentivise companies to build clean, efficient factories. Results took some time to appear, until quite recently, because the EU had allocated too many carbon credits and set the price too low. There was also little trading of the credits that were allocated. The market did not function. Now, the price has gone up, and the EU also introduced a mechanism to reduce the overall emissions cap, year on year. That causes the price to rise more, thereby incentivising all manufacturers to reduce their emissions. Slowly but surely, the emissions-trading system seemed to start working. The market is functioning.

We have taken great strides in a short time, and the notion of sustainability has expanded further in the first decades of the 21st century. Now, people often talk about *three* types of sustainability: *environmental* sustainability, *social* sustainability and *economic* (or financial) sustainability. Now, suddenly, economics is part of the game. We can see a link to our field. Ecology and sustainability are suddenly about much more than just not poisoning the white-tailed eagles. Politicians, business leaders and opinion-makers have started presenting their visions of the future in the form of three circles symbolising *environmental, social* and *economic* sustainability. The three circles are often depicted as overlapping and equal in size. The challenge is balancing these three aspects of sustainability. Which carries the greatest weight? In practice, the economic segment is often a bit bigger. This view of sustainability is about finding a balance between economic interests and other interests – weighing them up against each other, for and against. *We can't just think about the economy; we have to think about the environment as well.* It starts to feel like juggling, keeping a lot of balls in the air.

It's like sitting aboard a huge, creaking oil tanker that's difficult to manoeuvre. As is so often the case, the problem is knowledge. It's hard to get the oil tanker to change course as an individual consumer or buyer. Even if you make many small green choices, you will rarely get a glimpse of the consequences of your actions, even if you want to. If prices do not reflect the total cost of a product or service on the planet, we get lost in a maelstrom of information that even specialists find difficult to understand. Tricky.

Besides, some of us might want to let our own cows graze a little more on the commons and have the others pay. Sure, there might be a little less grass for other people's cows, but they won't notice. Will they? How can we solve the problem on our commons?

Policymakers refer to really tricky problems as *wicked problems*. These are problems that are difficult or even impossible to solve through existing means. They change over time and have no clear boundaries.

The solution depends on how a problem is defined, but we do not really know what the problem is. Stakeholders have differing world views and different frames for understanding the problem. An example of a wicked problem is how to achieve continued economic growth within our planet's limits. Climate change has been termed a *super wicked problem*, because it has the additional characteristic of a time limit for finding a solution. The clock appears to be ticking, like in a speed-chess game.

This is roughly where we're at, right now. We can *theoretically* control environmental destruction, provided we put the right price on environmental capital. That's not easy to do. But *if* we can do that, the price will lead us to set the right priorities. Note that this is a market economy, not a laissez-faire economy. Governments and international organisations have a clear role. For example, they can organise emissions-trading systems to set a cap on total acceptable emission levels, thereby forming the legislative framework.

A more revolutionary economic-environmental view that has quietly started to gather support is the idea that it is impossible to *balance* environmental capital against economic capital. They are completely different things. Apples and oranges. They are not substitutable. Environmental problems cannot be weighed against increased economic growth. Nor can they be offset by it. This debate is still underway, including at global climate summits. Developing countries, such as India, say that they need to keep burning coal as they build their economies. They have to be able to balance their economic growth against increased emissions. Of course, that is wrong, if you believe that environmental capital and economic capital are two distinct things that are not substitutable. In defence of India and many other developing countries, their per capita CO_2 emissions are far lower than those of Western countries. And they have no historical carbon debt going back 200 years. But there is no clear answer. A wicked problem indeed.

In purely practical terms, it is still extremely difficult to achieve economic and political buy-in to choices that generate fast results. It is not economically feasible. In the first chapter, we mentioned the difference between the cost of continuing to emit CO_2 and the cost of avoiding emissions. You may recall the British economist Nicholas Stern, who put a price on climate change. His report, *The Stern Review*, was commissioned by the British government under Gordon Brown. It spurred the debate on climate threat when it was published in 2006. Stern calculated that it was much cheaper to halt climate change now than to let it continue. Measures to stop climate change would cost 1% of global GDP. Waiting could cost up to 20% of global GDP.

It was like a faraway rumble, a vaguely concerning grey storm cloud in the distance on a summer's day. Do you really think it's coming this way? Looks to me like it's standing still. The sky seems such an innocent blue right above us. Let's just lie here in the sun a bit longer. If it starts to rain, we can grab our towels and make a dash for the car.

We'll be all right. Did you feel a raindrop? Nah.

Would you like some coffee? I've got homemade cookies.

We now have a new diagram to depict the link between the ecosystem and the economic system. It looks like a wedding cake. The bottom tier represents nature and environmental sustainability. On top of that is a smaller tier, which represents social sustainability. On top of that, resting on the other two tiers, is economic sustainability. The idea is that the economy is a small part of the ecosystem. The economy is not a ball that can be weighed up against another ball representing nature. They are all connected as parts of the same cake. The economy is a small system within the larger ecosystem. The economy is part of our society. Society is part of the ecosystem or biosphere. The economy is not abstract, although it might seem that way. Economic processes are ultimately also physical, chemical and biological processes.

As usual, it's the *externalities* that mess things up – the factors that usually have no cost and no price. They exist outside the things we are calculating. An environmental economist might also say that the marginal environmental cost of producing more goods has gone through the roof, increased exponentially, up to infinity. The ceiling is the critical limit of what the planet can bear. The term for this is *planetary boundaries.*

The British economist Kate Raworth added a floor to the planetary ceiling. The result was a doughnut. In between the ceiling for economic activity that is determined by the planetary boundaries for emissions, and the floor – defined as the lowest acceptable standard for things like housing, education, income, food and health – is where we can live. Between the social floor and the environmental ceiling. Not too much room, but not too little either. Just right. Like Goldilocks.

The sweet spot.

The innovative twist in Kate Raworth's doughnut model is that, unlike traditional economic theory, it does not attempt to maximise anything. More is not better. Enough is best. Nor is her model an optimisation of something that is measurable in units – in a price. There are many targets and boundaries all together. It's complicated.

Cake or doughnut?

A tough choice for an ape that likes more of everything. Maybe both?

Next stop, the bakery economy.

A LITTLE HAPPINESS

In which we consider
why wealthy people are often
portrayed as evil, and whether
more money really makes
you happier – and if so,
how much money is best?

HAPPINESS EXISTS.
We all know that.

And yet nobody really knows what happiness is. There is no easily accessible algorithm for happiness. Nor is there any generally accepted definition of happiness. You can only experience it. We also don't know the location of happiness within us. Our happiness centre cannot be captured on camera. Happiness is simply something big and important, yet also difficult and inaccessible.

That's not an unusual combination, in our lives.

Alongside the question of the meaning of life, and the question of what is true, happiness is one of the questions that has eternally occupied philosophical heavyweights.

Money – or, more accurately, our perpetual trading and exchanging – which is the glue holding this book together, plays a part in creating happiness. Or it plays a part in creating some of what we call happiness, up to a point. There are patterns to be found in our actions here, too.

If we go back to our first made-up example with the apes, they each had just one item: figs or nuts. Nothing else. Then they realised they could trade things with one another, and suddenly it happened. Having both figs and nuts was better than having just figs or nuts. That's the big secret – if it ever was a secret to begin with. Having two things to choose from in your pantry is better than having only one thing, and no choice. It's doesn't take much deep philosophical thought to reach that insight; most of us realise it instinctively. Fish and vegetables is better than only fish or only vegetables. Variety beats monotony in most situations. That's why we are so keen to carry on trading. We want to do it again and again. That leads us to conclude that more *options* generally lead to greater perceived happiness, for primates as well as people.

We might regard that matter as settled. There are, of course, as ever, special cases where we can drown in all the choices and options available. Greater choice increases the opportunity for happiness, but that is drowned in the unhappiness generated by the need to go through and evaluate a huge range of alternatives. But that's one of the many special cases in ultra-modern life. It's also something we will return to later.

Clearly, money per se is not what creates happiness. Money is just the means to enable other things to be traded. It's more the *opportunity* to acquire something in exchange that's the real happiness mechanism. Having not just figs or nuts, but both at the same time. Having not just leisure, but *work*, and therefore being able to exchange part of your time for money. And then, in the next step, exchanging part of your money for whatever you think you might need. For some people, food. For others, a glass of wine or a bicycle. And that's what's so great about money: it gives you a bit more freedom to shape your life the way you want. Happiness about having more money is happiness about knowing you have a bit more freedom to do things. More choices have entered the range of possibility. On a more fundamental level, of course, you can be happy about having more money because now you don't have to worry about how you're going to pay all your bills at the end of the month. You're in the black, with a bit of a safety cushion.

But, in everything from fairy tales to films and books, we are given a different picture. Over and over again, we are told that money sucks.

Money doesn't make anyone happy. Quite the opposite: money is a source of unhappiness. And not only that. Money also seems to have something to do with its owners being – or eventually becoming – evil.

In everything from the New Testament in the Bible, which says that excessive interest in money is a deadly sin, to Midas in Greek myth and Gordon Gekko in Hollywood's *Wall Street*, wealthy people and those interested in money are often portrayed as loathsome figures.

There are plenty of examples from books and popular culture. Just look at George Costanza, the neurotic cheapskate in the US sitcom *Seinfeld*, or Donald Duck's grumpy uncle, Scrooge McDuck. There's also the dastardly businessman Mr Burns in *The Simpsons*. And of course the iconic miser Ebenezer Scrooge in Dickens's *A Christmas Carol*.

There are many more examples, but we can draw a preliminary conclusion from these: in the vast majority of cases, awful people (or creatures) are conjured up when there is money in the picture. These characters are not the sort of folks you'd want to hang around with. As usual, though, there are exceptions. Just consider glamorous superheroes like Batman, or even James Bond. They seem to have 'enough' cash for it not to be a problem – an invisible fortune somewhere in the background. But, usually, money is presented as something incompatible with being a good person. Many myths show money and wealth in abundance bringing various disasters in its wake. The problem is that most of these images of wealth aren't realistic. In the real world, there doesn't seem to be a rule that says having access to money guarantees unhappiness. This is an issue that has been studied and investigated to an almost ridiculous degree by sociologists, psychologists and of course economists. People from all these disciplines are interested in the question of whether or not money really makes people happier.

A clear pattern emerges from this tidal wave of literature and scholarly articles. For us, in this part of the world, and in the 21st century, happiness increases along with income up to somewhere in the region of €5,000 to €7,000 per month. Approximately.

Before tax. But then, for most people, slowly but surely, as income increases further, happiness levels off.

These figures are approximate. Differences between countries, in everything from currency exchange rates to living standards and inflation, will affect the exact figures. The dividing line will obviously be different in war-torn Ukraine and well-heeled Luxembourg. That level of €5,000 is an approximate figure for an industrialised country like Sweden. Most people get a real buzz when they go from a student budget to a monthly salary. In fact, many who remember living in student accommodation and watching every penny would say the first months of being paid a monthly salary were a time of sheer, unadulterated happiness.

Less instant noodles. More hearty dinners. The feeling of being in charge of your own life and eating something really nice.

When someone gets a new job and their monthly pay packet goes from €2,500 to €3,000, that's a buzz. It's a noticeable change. When that person goes from €4,200 a month to €5,000, it also hits the happiness button.

But then things level off pretty quickly. You don't get the same buzz from another €1,000. And, if another €1,000 turns up, it's even less of a rush. It's a bit more cash to jingle around, and the extra money generates a bit of happiness, but not as much as before. Marginal happiness levels in our part of the world decrease significantly when salaries exceed €5,000 per month. A decrease in marginal happiness means that the happiness graph increases more and more slowly, eventually levelling off.

So we know that more money makes us happier, up to a certain point – at the individual level. Meanwhile, most economists and other thinkers agree that money on a macro level – a country's GDP, for instance – is a very blunt instrument for measuring happiness. Or for measuring prosperity and development. There are a number of reasons for this. Our pursuit of happiness is a key part of our existence, and it is related in some way to our finances. But the link between the way we measure economic success per person in a whole country and happiness is unclear.

This is because GDP is a measure of economic *activity*. That is to say, *quantity* (the amount of activity) and not *quality* (whether it is good or bad). All economic activity is counted as a positive contribution, regardless of whether we would label any particular events as *good* or *bad*. Building new schools, being able to afford more food or a bigger sofa, or improving our healthcare increases GDP. But so do negative events like war or earthquakes, if they generate new jobs, costly rescue operations or vast rebuilding programmes.

From our own biological viewpoint, it is also deceptive that GDP does not measure a lot of things that are good for our health and long-term happiness, particularly everything that happens in the environment. There is no increase in GDP if the natural world thrives. Nor is there a decrease in GDP if there is an oil spill or a finite resource runs out, such as an animal species or two. As long as trees remain standing, they are economically invisible, even though they give us air, shade and other good things. *Natural* activity is not reflected in GDP. But, if we chop a tree down, GDP will increase. Tricky.

A nation's GDP also says nothing about how money is distributed within the country. Even if economic growth is high, you and I probably won't be happy if neither of us attains that 50,000 kronor a month. That would mean GDP went up but our personal situation remained unchanged. Or worse. Or maybe the GDP increased because some madman was constantly blowing up schools, hospitals and old people's homes. That would lead to an unprecedented construction boom, plus a labour shortage and rising wages in certain sectors. But it would not make our lives better overall, nor would it make us happier – quite the reverse, as people would have died.

Since people realised GDP is of little use for measuring quality of life, various attempts – some serious, others less so – have been made to come up with another measure to use instead of or alongside it. It's no easy task. We can experience happiness, but how can we measure it? Presumably, every country has wondered the same thing at some point. The United Nations Development Programme (UNDP) launched its Human Development Index (HDI) in 1990, combining factors like average lifespan, education levels and gross national income. A life is so much more than just trading. But, even here, we are still a good way away from measuring what we call happiness.

Nevertheless, most countries still measure their economic growth in terms of GDP. It remains the slightly crude thermometer we reach for to check the patient's condition. And it remains at the centre of business and financial journalism.

GDP, inflation, unemployment: in practice, these three indicators are the figures we use to measure a nation's happiness. They answer the question, *How is our economy doing?* and so they indirectly answer the question of how *we're* doing. It's hard to teach an old dog new tricks. The old dogs remember that economic development plays a big role in the beginning, when a country or region is pulling itself out of poverty. It works the same way for individual people. The first extra boost in pay gives a bigger increase in happiness than the last, marginal one.

So, GDP doesn't record whether our health gets better or worse, if we live longer or have cleaner air, or if we actually get happier. It only measures the *amount* of economic activity. For most of the 20th century, the link between increasing economic activity, reduced poverty and rising wages was so clear that we could ignore the shortcomings of GDP as a yardstick. Basically, *more* meant the same as *better*. And doesn't more of everything usually make us happy?

We will find that there is a long history of searching for a way to measure happiness, trying to come up with the right method. Neither GDP nor HDI was the first attempt. In fact, they were quite late to the party, coming behind a long line of thinkers trying to work out the nature of happiness and whether it can be captured in figures somehow.

Once again, we return to our history, philosophical questions and morality. It is no accident that Adam Smith, the man often called the first economist, regarded himself as a moral philosopher. Our attitude to money is somehow related to our attitude to happiness, morality and the meaning of life – philosophy, in other words – and definitely to the question of what happiness really is.

The question of measuring happiness in economics has played a central role in the rise of economics as a social science. If we look into this further, we end up back with the British chaps in the late 18th and 19th century. They were all near the centre of the global economy at the time: England – the birthplace of the Industrial Revolution.

Those British fellows only talked indirectly about happiness, though. Their favourite word was *utility*. Their group came to be known as *utilitarians*. They sought an answer to the question of how we should organise society to create the greatest possible utility for the greatest number of people – a reasonable question for a society in upheaval as the long-established agrarian way of life was pushed aside by factories and urbanisation. If a unit of measurement for utility could be found, it would be possible to add up the utility from individuals into a total utility for a city or even a whole country. By comparing the total utility for various alternatives, you could figure out which was the best. The total amount of happiness would be maximised.

One of the first to add this to the mix was Jeremy Bentham, a British philosopher. In 1789, the year of the French Revolution, he published a book in which he proposed a method of calculating pleasure or pain.

Nowadays, we might call it a happiness-maximising algorithm. Does that term sound familiar? Algorithms are used in social media and determine the content that appears on your phone – all to increase utility for users. This is the same idea that was used back then, although plenty of people think that online companies' algorithms do anything *but* generate utility. Especially on the societal level.

Bentham maintained that morality is a function of the pleasure or pain arising from an action. In order to calculate the value of a particular pleasure or pain, he proposes seven variables to consider:

- Intensity
- Duration
- Certainty or uncertainty (how certain are you of what will happen?)
- Propinquity or remoteness (how close or far away is it in relation to a person or people?)
- Fecundity (how likely is the experience to be followed by sensations of the same kind?)
- Purity (what are the chances of the experience not being followed by experiences of the opposite kind?)
- Extent (how many people are affected?)

Then, all the factors are combined into a single experience. It's the totality that matters. Not an easy task in practice, but no problem in theory. Bentham invented a unit of measurement for pleasure and called it the *hedon*. Pain could be measured in units of *dolor*. If your action produces more hedons than dolors, go for it! Having come this far in his thinking, Bentham seems to notice things are getting tricky. He has made it into philosophy's heavyweight category. He supplements his calculations with a little poem that includes all his variables:

> Intense, long, certain, speedy, fruitful, pure—
> Such marks in pleasures and in pains endure.
> Such pleasures seek if private be thy end:
> If it be public, wide let them extend

Such pains avoid, whichever be thy view:
If pains must come, let them extend to few.

If you memorise the poem, you can recall all the factors to weigh up in making a moral decision. It's a self-help ditty. Helpful at every fork in the road. Has our ape been transformed into an eccentric British philosopher who adds up hedons and dolors?

Bentham's self-help poem seems a bit silly to us now. It's not as common to use poems or rhymes as memory aids these days. We've usually got a smartphone handy. But the truth is that our world is a far more Benthamite world than the one Jeremy Bentham lived in. For example, we are forced to make more choices, both large and small, than ever. A modern city-dweller makes several thousand choices every day. And we do make a sort of utility calculation, whether consciously or not. There are hedons and dolors all around, for us 21st-century people.

Bentham's ideas inspired many successors. His idea of a calculus of utility – an algorithm – sowed the seeds for our present-day view of the economy. Neoclassical economic theory arose in the late 19th century: a powerful bundle of theories, which have steered economic and political discourse, particularly in the most recent four decades. So, the versifying Bentham's ideas extend right into our lives here and now. Ideas about how free-market forces and increased consumer power optimise utility flourished in the Western world in the 1980s. The main standard-bearers were the UK's prime minister Margaret Thatcher and her chum, US president Ronald Reagan.

The notions of Thatcher and Reagan about the best means and sources of creating utility would impact the entire world from the 1980s onward. But what is this neoclassical economic theory all about? And how did we get there? It's important to take a thorough approach here. Let's start from the beginning. If there is a *neo*classical economic theory, there must also be a *classical* theory – an original that was later updated. *Classical* economic theory refers primarily to the ideas of a group of 18th-and 19th-century British thinkers. We have already met a couple of them: our old friend Adam Smith, the first economist, and Jeremy Bentham, inventor of the happiness equation. But there were many others too.

These men attempted to explain prosperity and economic growth. It's not surprising that the topic attracted their attention at that time and place. Industrialisation had just begun to transform the world, and England was where it all started. One important question concerned the actual source of a product's value. Another question was about income: labour, land and capital generated different types of income. Labour produced income in the form of wages; land could be leased out; and capital generated interest income. Karl Marx, the granddaddy of communism, could be termed a classical economist. He wrote more than he calculated. He philosophised and moralised. And he was convinced it was workers' input, and nothing else, that determined the true value of goods. But we are not going to spend too much time on the classics here. Our present-day economic system has been shaped primarily by a different, more recent, bundle of economic theories. The underlying ideas for these theories were formulated in the late 19th century and acquired the name *neoclassical*.

Once again, we encounter British men with extravagant sideburns. Their theories place greater importance on the role of individuals' *demand* as a fundamental driver of the economy. We are assumed to act in a vast free market to maximise our own utility, so we are looking at society from an individual viewpoint. The market's choices are the sum total of individuals' choices. Society's interests are determined by individuals' aggregate interests. Maximising pleasure and minimising pain. Utilitarianism is back, just in a new wrapper.

The main difference is that the later sideburns said that your costs are irrelevant for pricing. The price of goods depends on what a buyer or buyers are prepared to pay, and something is worth whatever someone wants to pay for it. Full stop. Whether anyone wants to produce and sell the goods for that price is an entirely different question. In this view, nothing has any objective value *beyond* what someone is willing to pay for it. It therefore follows that the price, funnily enough, is *always* the right price. The price can never be wrong, because it is set at the intersection between supply and demand. You can think of it as a sort of constant auction, where all the world's prices are set. As we all know, the price at an auction is always the right price. The neoclassicists assume that all our resources are thus efficiently allocated in society by the magical price. Everything is allocated according to buyers' demand.

The value of a good – that is, what someone is willing to pay for it – is assumed to reflect our own preferences. We are assumed to be not only intelligent and well informed, but also entirely rational, perfectly informed beings. That assumption turned out to be quite far removed from our true nature. As for companies, they are assumed to seek to maximise their profit at all times. In other words, there are a large number of assumptions and theoretical models underlying the conclusions drawn by the neoclassical economists. The term *Homo economicus* – the economic human – was coined to describe people in this model. Always rational, possessing perfect information. *We are the robots.*

Based on our perfect information, we make rational choices regarding what to spend our hard-earned money on. And because resources are always scarce in neoclassical economics, we want to make the right choice. Our desire and ability to pay for a good or service – known as demand – determines what is produced and what it is worth. It is the right choice. Ultimately, it is the individual's choice that sets the agenda in the neoclassical whisker-wearers' proposed world.

This whole mechanism functions best in an entirely free market, where the state does not get involved in prices. If the state does get involved, according to the neoclassicists, prices will be distorted and the wrong things will be prioritised. If taxes and fees are added to a price, then that price no longer reflects individuals' wishes. That's all perfectly logical, even though we now know that things can easily be the other way round in the real world: there is a desire and need to control demand for certain things, such as alcohol and cigarettes. Humans are far from rational; nor do we have perfect information for the choices we make. If we did, presumably the demand for cigarettes would be close to zero.

But let's stay in our theoretical world for a bit longer. Neoclassical economic theory focuses on the optimal allocation of our resources. The starting point is that all commodities in the economy are limited. We start from a position of scarcity, so we have to choose the best path forward. Our choices depend on our preferences. For example, we choose how much to work based on our preferences for money or leisure – similar to Jeremy Bentham's pleasure versus pain, hedon versus dolor.

Another important concept from the neoclassicists' bundle of theories that gained huge influence is the idea of *marginal utility*. The first cup of coffee gives you a great deal of pleasure; the second cup gives you somewhat less. And so on. You are not prepared to pay as much for the fifth cup of the day as you were for the first. The marginal utility decreases. And this applies to everything. You have seen similar logic applied earlier in this chapter. Happiness at earning more money increases more slowly as your income approaches 50,000 kronor per month. Even money, that made-up commodity, displays decreasing marginal utility.

As the neoclassicists entered the scene, something else happened that would give many of the world's economics students ulcers. It is an idea that alienates most people from economic thinking concerning greater or lesser utility – namely, the entry of mathematics into economics. Economists hoped to develop more precise tools to help them evaluate various alternative actions. Economics went from being a branch of philosophy to a quantitative social science. The discipline was previously called *political economy*, but now it started to go by the more neutral name of *economics*. The neoclassicists created the famous diagrams with supply and demand curves that cross in the middle. If you're going to use maths to study happiness, you need to be able to measure utility or happiness. Thus we can say that economics became a mathematical form of social science. Philosophising and moralising of the kind we saw among the early muttonchops-wearers were later replaced by measurements and calculations.

Somewhere along the way, Bentham's units of hedon and dolor gave way to setting a value on goods. That is, what people are willing to pay. The subjective theory of value requires no assessment of pleasure or pain. We just need to determine the price. Of course, this implies indirectly that a rich person's utility is regarded as greater than a poor person's, because a rich person can place a higher value on goods. But we can ignore this minor complaint if we just look at each individual's choices. From the individual's perspective, in the choice between two alternatives, the economic valuation reflects the goods' perceived utility.

The word *utility* is used in a rhetorical manner here. It sounds like something useful, or something you can utilise. But *utility* can also mean that an individual values sweets or a gram of drugs more highly than vegetables or a nutritious three-course meal. *Utility* does not have to be useful or beneficial for an individual, in terms of being good for their health. *Utility* doesn't need to be good for society either, in terms of promoting public health, education or justice. In economic theory, *maximum utility* is a self-explanatory term. It is simply the sum of all individuals' free choices. And, if their choices really are free and reflect individuals' preferences, utility will be maximised.

Maximising happiness. Minimising suffering.

As you will notice, a great deal of individual freedom and self-determination is baked into this theory. That is the core of liberalism. The starting point is the notion that the individual – and no one else – knows best what they want to do with their money, their life and their health. No state, authority or organisation should determine what is best and provides the greatest utility.

One criticism of utilitarianism as an idea and a philosophy, apart from its economic application, is that it does not take fairness *between* individuals or individual people's right to life and freedom into account. If a group of individuals' happiness increases when one person lives in slavery and misery, that can be counted as maximising happiness. That's an extreme example to show that it is not a straightforward matter to total up every individual's happiness to arrive at the total happiness of a society. But there are more criticisms to come.

As we know, Karl Marx was hung up on *capital*. He also wrote from the centre of the British Empire. Marx was German, but he did his work at the British Museum Library in London – at more or less the same time as the neoclassicists were assembling their economic theories in other British libraries. Here was yet another man, and one very keen on facial hair. He was also an economist who one could say acquired a certain political significance, to put it mildly. Entire countries and blocs were restructured according to Marx's ideas. Economists are not just obscure theorists who argue in libraries and classrooms. Some, like John

Stuart Mill with liberalism, and Karl Marx with Marxism, can initiate entire ideologies that change the world. They can also serve as advisers to politicians, or teachers and mentors to the advisers – the ones who influence political discourse and affect all of our lives.

So, neoclassical ideas about free markets and their benefits have been particularly strong and influential over the past four decades. They were implemented in the former Eastern-Bloc states and the Soviet Union as a sort of shock therapy after the fall of the Berlin Wall, and hastened globalisation. They encouraged nearly every country to deregulate and streamline many of their markets. The idea was a simple one: namely, that we needed to get functioning marketplaces up and running as quickly as possible, where individuals could exercise choice. The sooner the better.

After all, we are looking for happiness. But the idea that happiness will come to us via wonderfully free markets has not always held such appeal. That sort of thinking had spent a lot of time on the scrap heap. After the massive stock-market crash of 1929 and the Great Depression in the 1930s, the idea that free markets were a good thing was a hard sell. Free markets had led to a tidal wave of companies going bust, armies of jobless people and, ultimately, a world war. Demand was low, to say the least. Instead, ideas blossomed about various types of state intervention in the economy. This is when a British economist and bohemian by the name of John Maynard Keynes entered the picture. An out-of-the-ordinary man with original ideas, he was not as convinced as the old moustachioed chaps that the market always knew best. Keynes would lend his name to a whole school of economic thought, known as Keynesianism.

Towards the end of the Second World War, Keynes travelled to the conference held at the luxury Bretton Woods resort in New Hampshire and took part in negotiations for the new international monetary management system. Along with other treaties such as GATT (General Agreement on Tariffs and Trade), it spurred economies back into action after the war. Time was short. There was a lot of building to be done, and fast. Most Western countries were receptive to Keynes's ideas about an active state that stimulates and guides the market economy by means of various investment and support packages. The free market needed to

be harnessed and managed – as long as prosperity and happiness were the ultimate goal, that is.

But the system that believed in competition got some competition of its own. On the other side of the Iron Curtain, under the Soviet Union's overriding authority, planned economies were upheld as the way to achieve rapid industrialisation: rapid economic growth without free markets. Planned economies might already have been developing cracks, but it was not apparent to all outside observers just then; the signs in the skies indicated otherwise. On 4 October 1957, the Soviet Union became the first country in the world to send a little device into space to orbit the Earth. The little satellite, called Sputnik – which means 'travelling companion' in Russian – served as evidence that all that business about free markets was not the only possible way to build a modern society. When the USSR sent a dog called Laika into space soon after – and the United States countered by sending a monkey into space – more people than ever before realised a race was on between two fundamentally different ways of structuring lives and societies.

This was a competition between two systems: the Soviets' centrally planned economy standing in opposition to Keynes and the neoclassicists' ideas about free individuals making their own choices. Then as now, symbolic acts and media images played a part. The first monkeys the Americans sent into space did not survive, but then, in May 1959, a monkey called Baker made it back to Earth after nine minutes of weightlessness in space. A few years later, the Soviets managed to send the first person into space – before the USA. Then a race ensued to be the first to reach the Moon. Ultimately, it was a fierce, intense rivalry between two systems. And space travel was just one field of endeavour where the two systems competed head to head.

Two ideas about the route to happiness.

Which one would bring glad tidings to everyone?

In the years after the Second World War, many countries in the Western world, and particularly in Europe, were experiencing almost unprecedented growth. The idea of the welfare state could be implemented. Sweden and the other Nordic countries showed the way. We built factories. We built houses. We built schools. We bought cars, campervans and summer cottages. We built motorways. We built apartment buildings. The houses and apartments were warm and comfortable, heated with oil-fired boilers. Everything chugged along nicely, alongside the assembly lines.

The Americans put their astronauts on the Moon in 1969 – and got them back home again. The USA took a brief lead in the space race. A man on the Moon! Now there shouldn't be any doubt about which societal model could deliver. Putting a man on the Moon and flying him home again, in good shape, was a great triumph for the Western model of organising a nation's economy and society. But then, in 1973, the oil crisis struck. Another oil crisis came along a few years later. Petroleum prices went up, and people's trust in the dominant mixed economic model went down. Way down. Western Europe and the United States suffered from persistent inflation and rising unemployment.

We weren't so happy anymore, here in the West.

Meanwhile, in the Eastern-bloc countries, it had become obvious that centrally planned economies could not deliver material standards in the long term to match what the West's market economies had achieved. Even taking the oil crises and inflation into account, Western living standards were higher. Much higher. Anyone visiting an Eastern-bloc country could see for themselves. Shop shelves stood empty, and queues snaked outside any shops that did have goods in stock. Similarly, the quality of goods produced in planned economies always seemed inferior. Nobody was queuing up in Western countries to buy Soviet jeans. In the USSR, though, you could sell worn-out American jeans for high prices.

Something was seriously wrong in the planned economies. People were clearly not too happy in the East. But they couldn't even complain openly. Without exception, planned economies were always paired with oppression and totalitarian regimes of one hue or another. But we will leave those matters aside for now, important as they are. Free-market economies can also be combined with oppression and totalitarian regimes, unfortunately.

The neoclassicists were waiting in the wings for their chance to make a comeback. That's exactly what they did – in a big way. We needed to return to an economy with the optimal conditions for creating the most happiness. The turnaround would be led by the highly educated daughter of an English shopkeeper. Her name was Margaret Thatcher. During her term as prime minister, a number of economic ideas – which we recognise as originating with neoclassical thinkers – gained ground in many countries. These principles went on a world tour, much like a rock band, starting around 1980. One country after another adopted a list of principles, like a sort of mantra.

- Rules prevent the economy from performing optimally. Set the *invisible hand* free. The market must be free. *Deregulate.* Streamline.
- Trade within and between countries should be free. Free trade replaces regulated trade. Tariffs are reduced. Other trade barriers in the form of national regulations and standards are dismantled wherever possible.
- Excessive taxes also distort the market. Lower taxes are preferable to higher taxes. Individuals and businesses are better than the state at investing resources where they are needed. The term *tax burden* is introduced. It expresses how taxes act as a drag on businesses and individuals. In many countries, including Sweden, the tax system is reformed. Taxes are reduced on employment income to stimulate employment. Taxes are reduced on capital gains to stimulate investment.
- For the same reasons as above, private companies are regarded as more efficient than public bodies. Many public-sector industries, companies, authorities and organisations are privatised. In Sweden, even parts of the school system are later privatised.
- Private ownership is viewed as a right.

In some countries – though not Sweden or most of the EU – trade unions were also discouraged, using reasoning from neoclassical economics. Unions were seen as a form of regulation of the labour market – interference – which prevented the economy from functioning optimally. The thesis held that free markets always provide the best possible results for society.

Margaret Thatcher launched a major offensive against British trade unions. Similar efforts were made in the USA and elsewhere around the world.

The ideological world tour continued, taking free-market reforms to one country after another. Major international bodies, such as the World Bank and the World Trade Organization, advocated policies based on neoclassical theory. Implementation of these market reforms was a condition placed on countries, if they wanted to borrow money.

There was one area – which can be measured in numbers – where the reforms seemed to work very well. Global international trade increased, and the numbers kept accelerating. Trade increased tenfold in the period between 1950 and 1990. That's no mean feat. Then trade increased the same amount in just one decade, from 1990 to 2000. And again, in *less* than ten years after 2000 – despite finance crises in 2001 and 2008. World trade then underwent the same increase again in less than ten years, despite a long, crippling eurozone crisis, long-term unemployment and global austerity packages imposed by the World Bank. Trade between the countries of the world has been spiralling upwards, with a fortyfold increase between 1950 and 2020. Never before has so much prosperity been generated for so many people in such a short time. In the early 2020s, talk increased of the elimination of poverty. If anything meant happiness, surely that was it?

Not everything was a bed of roses, though. Some of the new ideas promised stability. According to the theory, free markets should naturally move towards a state of equilibrium. But that equilibrium seemed to have a bit of trouble establishing itself. Instead, the economy teetered and crashed every so often – in 1991, 1997, 2001, 2008 and 2010. It's actually the stock markets that crashed, but they dragged the rest of the economy down with them. Such crises also seem difficult to predict. The system appears to be turbulent, rather than one that seeks an equilibrium. We end up paying a high price for free financial markets.

All of the utility-maximising, pleasure-seeking individuals rush in the same direction at the same time. First one way, then the other. New technology adds fuel to this herd behaviour. Of course, the chaps in 19th-century London couldn't have foreseen a computer or phone in every person's hand. Inventions are always hard to foresee.

It was clear that we could rock this massive boat. Overconfidence started to give way to uncertainty. Could we have overlooked something? Questions started to pile up.

Do we really act rationally as individuals? Do we have perfect information? Is price really a good measure of what we prefer? If so, are individuals' preferences a good measure of what is good for society as a whole? And, above all, is it really possible to add up every individual's wishes to determine what's best for the public?

All the neoclassicists' ideas were based on a large number of assumptions. *Homo economicus.* An image emerges of a gigantic elephant of economic policy balancing on a small inflatable ball of theoretical assumptions.

It's a funny image. But is that really the right way to happiness?

Happiness, at least in the form of economic prosperity, is also rather unevenly distributed in this model. It stresses that the state should not get involved and redistribute income; the distribution of economic resources is best handled by the market. If our GDP grows, sooner or later happiness will trickle down to everyone. That's what the theory says. If company directors and entrepreneurs make more money, so will everybody else. The idea is that everybody will be better off. Sooner or later.

But income distribution is not the only thing that raises questions. The link between high GDP and high happiness levels for everyone is still unclear.

Just look at the USA. A survey showed that while GDP had increased throughout the post-Second World War era – tripling, in fact – happiness levels remained fairly constant. Americans seemed to have been happiest right after the war, in the 1940s and 1950s. Maybe they were happy to be living in peace? There could have been some other reason, too. Taxes or income distribution might also have played a part. That was a time when the USA had high marginal tax rates, with a relatively large redistribution of income. Perhaps people were happy about reduced stratification in society? The answer is not obvious, even though we can see statistical correlations.

GDP continued to grow in the USA between 1980 and 2020, but the growth rate started to slow in the West. Meanwhile, the wealthiest segment of the population saw their wealth increase significantly. It was not as simple as salaries for bank directors rising more than for ordinary middle-class jobs (though they did in fact do so). Above all, the increase was due to the greater ease of earning money from capital. People who already have money can purchase property or shares and make more money from their capital. In the post-war era, capital growth was three times greater than GDP growth, which meant by definition that wealthy people's share of the economy grew.

Behind this development was an economic theory that wealthy people should be allowed to get really rich – for several reasons. Partly so they would have sufficient capital to invest in the economy, such as by starting businesses to create more jobs and greater prosperity, and partly because the people who invest ought to be properly rewarded and encouraged to invest more. Thus wealth would trickle down from the wealthy to the less well-off masses. The theory was dubbed *trickle-down economics*.

It's worth remembering that economic and political theorists enjoy thought experiments, assumptions, equations and abstract reasoning. These are theoretical models we're discussing – a simplified picture of the world. A map. The reasoning works inside the model. But, if you look at the real world, it might not.

A frequently cited riddle from game theory is known as 'The Prisoner's Dilemma.' The scenario is as follows. Two prisoners are being kept in separate cells. They cannot communicate with each other. If they both stay silent, they will receive a short sentence of six months. The police offer each one a deal, in which he will be released if he squeals on his co-defendant. Each risks a more severe sentence of ten years if the other prisoner gives evidence against him while he himself remains silent. If each gives evidence against the other, they will both be sentenced to two years. The safest strategy to ensure a fairly light sentence is to squeal. So they both squeal, and both are sentenced to two years.

Conclusion: self-interest is always the best strategy. That is, it is always rational for an individual to act out of self-interest.

But our real-life experience tells us something different. The opposite, in fact. This is what makes this thought experiment so provocative and hard to accept. We know that people do not always act out of self-interest. In fact, people often display a strong desire to cooperate. We are there for one another, even in extreme situations. Besides, selfishness and self-interest are universally held in low regard.

Do unto others as you would have them do unto you, as the Golden Rule says. Or, as the playground version puts it: snitches get stitches.

Meanwhile, self-sacrifice – the opposite of self-interest – is almost always viewed approvingly.

How do these things fit together?

Enter evolution and the old ape inside us once more. We want to join the herd. We simply seem to be happier when we're part of a group, when we cooperate, than when we act selfishly and risk being excluded from the group. Part of the answer is that 'The Prisoner's Dilemma' is only played once. If you add a time element and play the game several times, the equation and conclusions change radically. Suddenly, it is far better to cooperate than to be selfish. If you know the other prisoner didn't squeal last time, you will trust him. And vice versa. Trust is valuable in a herd or society.

Trust is the foundation of what is called social sustainability. It's also the foundation of all economic exchange and increasing prosperity. We've seen how value is ultimately created by trading things. Without trust, there is no trade. Building a society requires an ape who is willing to exchange things, and who can do so without fear of being tricked. The trust you experience is based on your reputation.

So how does a profit-maximising individual ape act? Out of self-interest or not? Whose profit should be maximised? Their own, or the group's?

If individual self-interest means cooperating, does it then make sense to emphasise the individual?

What do you think, my fig-eating friend?

CURIOUSER AND CURIOUSER

In which the ape and capital
head out into cyberspace,
fall down a rabbit hole,
colonise the future and
trade in derivatives
and bitcoin.

Ultimately, money is about simplifying and improving our existence.

We have seen how our ape's life was improved and simplified when this particular made-up item came along. Money entered our lives as a sort of magical middleman, capable of transforming one thing into another. Potatoes can be transformed into a back massage. A basket of just-caught fish can be transformed into a couple of bottles of wine. It just takes a bit of faith – not in God or any other supreme being, just faith that others share the same belief. When there is a shared trust in money, everyone can cooperate. Nice and universal. But, if that trust vanishes or frays a tiny bit at the edges, problems arise. Everyone in the group has to be able to trust each other. As we will soon see, when our faith in money, its value and banking starts to wobble, disaster lurks around the corner. All it takes is for something, or some*one*, to give us a reason to doubt.

When Richard 'the Gorilla' Fuld filed for bankruptcy protection on behalf of his firm in the small hours of 15 September 2008, trust evaporated in an instant. All over the world. There is a Dutch saying that trust comes on foot but leaves on horseback. On this occasion, it left at a full gallop. That night, in New York, one of the world's largest banks – Lehman Brothers – suspended its payments. Richard Fuld would enter the history books as the last chairman and chief executive officer of Lehman Brothers, the bank that destabilised our entire economy. The world was plunged into the biggest financial crisis since the start of the Great Depression in 1929.

A long period of explosive growth in new ways for banks to manage money came to a terrifying end in the autumn of 2008. It quickly became clear that many of the world's banks were carrying far greater debt than laws or regulations allowed. Clever new ways of investing and paying out money had stretched the bounds of what was permissible and what was not. We have seen that banks need to hold a certain amount of capital in relation to what they lend. That reduces the risk of the bank going bust. But, with a bit of imagination, you can argue about what is your own capital and what is other people's. Besides, you can actually stretch your own capital. For example, how do you count any money the bank will receive in the future? Is it counted as part of the bank's capital right now? Can it be counted? Should it be? If everything goes according to plan, that money will become the bank's money someday. Problems arise when things don't go according to plan.

Crisis teams assembled and foreheads furrowed during the critical days and weeks after Lehman Brothers' bankruptcy. The world held its collective breath. The leaders of the world's largest economies agreed that trust in money and banks had to be preserved – without delay, no matter what the cost. If people around the world lost faith in money and banks, a complete global financial and societal collapse would be just around the corner. Suddenly, that universal system that enables everyone to cooperate, and allows us to exchange anything for anything else, might be gone. It would be comparable to losing our ability to speak to each other and having to go back to gesticulating. Old-fashioned bartering is not a functional alternative in a complex international community of nearly eight billion individuals.

We all want to avoid that sort of complete collapse. The consequences would be unthinkable. So the leaders of the world's major economies joined together in a unique effort, under extreme time pressure, to assemble a package of measures to guarantee that people's money would remain in their bank accounts and retain its value, even if a number of banks, both large and small, went bust.

The practical interventions to salvage trust varied from country to country. But one could sense a return of the superstar economist John Maynard Keynes. When the market fails, the state must step in – just as Keynes had advocated. Huge rescue packages and guarantee programmes were launched all over the world. China invested vast sums in infrastructure and other sectors to counteract the 2008–9 recession.

The notion that free markets alone could provide the best solutions took another huge hit – the biggest since 1929.

Ultimate responsibility for footing the bill and restoring faith in the economy fell to taxpayers. Banking and finance laws and regulations were also tightened up following lengthy negotiations to reach the third Basel Accord (also known as Basel III, named for the Swiss city where the negotiations took place). A number of negotiators, including Adair Turner, chairman of the UK's Financial Services Authority, wanted the new regulatory framework to go even further. Nevertheless, the new framework was a change. Everyone agreed that another threat to the entire global financial system could not be allowed to happen. We had come too close to the abyss. The rescue packages stabilised and calmed the most acute parts of the crisis. Everyone seemed to understand that the leaders of the world's largest economies were prepared to preserve trust in the banks and monetary system at nearly any price.

Well, maybe not everyone. Despite the rescue packages, Satoshi Nakamoto was still angry. He was furious. He was convinced he could rely on nothing and no one. He reached the same conclusion as many others in the 'cypherpunk' movement, a loose network of politically engaged technogeeks, academics and thinkers who had started meeting up in San Francisco in the early 1990s. They regarded governments, authority figures and legislation in general as the problem, not the solution.

In 1988, Timothy May – one of the movement's members – wrote in his *Crypto Anarchist Manifesto* that the objective was to undermine all forms of governmental authority and create a political order without laws, administrators or rulers – they couldn't be trusted. No governments, no borders, no taxes and no laws – that was the vision. So, what currency would fit into that version of the future?

In a unique act of cooperation, the nations of the world restored trust in money and the banking system. But that's only temporary. It's virtually certain we will soon face a new crisis. And then we'll be back in the same place: a crisis of trust, when most of us will experience the dizzying feeling for a moment that everything might collapse. Our savings gone, or worthless. Dreams shattering. That's something Satoshi Nakamoto did not want to go through again. And he felt that the banks and countries of the world were the source of the problem. They kept making the same mistake – printing too much money. Besides repeated banking crises, increasing the monetary supply also undermines the value of money. That means inflation. Like many other cypherpunks, Nakamoto thought that human shortcomings and self-interest were too embedded in the functioning of banks and government bodies to avoid the problem of repeated crises and inflation – within the established system, anyway. His conclusion was obvious. There needed to be a way of storing and transferring value completely out of the reach of banks and governments. In the autumn of 2008, he was ready to unveil his idea.

Maybe that's how it happened. But we don't really know. Nobody has actually met Satoshi Nakamoto. The name is a pseudonym for the one or more people who created bitcoin, by far the world's best-known crypto-currency. Cryptocurrency is an alternative system for storing and trans-ferring value outside the banking system, independent of any country. You can think of it as a kind of email for money. In a little over ten years, it reached the upper echelons of the finance world, having been men-tioned for the first time, on 31 October 2008, in an email from satoshi@gmx.com. The digital-only currency that was launched in 2009 based on those principles reached audiences far beyond the circle of libertarian cypherpunks who had been experimenting with various forms of digital money for several decades – usually without much success. Despite its flaws and risks, bitcoin has gone on to become a success and something of a phenomenon – a cryptocurrency rock star. It is the first modern curren-cy not to be controlled by any country, bank or other organisation, and therefore not affected by human whims or shortcomings. And, perhaps most importantly, the number of bitcoins can never exceed 21 million. Satoshi Nakamoto incorporated an upper limit in his creation. Thus there is no risk that eager bank directors or nervous central bank chiefs could spark inflation or undermine the currency's value. Just the way a true cypherpunk would have it.

Bitcoin was the first in a series of hundreds and then thousands of cryp-tocurrencies existing outside the world's system of banks and countries

– an entire ecosystem of competing currencies. This is just what the freedom-fetishising thinker Friedrich von Hayek recommended in his 1976 book *The Denationalisation of Money*. Let people and companies issue their own money, he said. In competition with one another. The most competitive will survive. It will be an effective way to avoid sticky-fingered governments issuing too much money and causing inflation. It is in the self-interest of private currency creators to avoid actions that would reduce the currency's value, according to Hayek.

Bitcoin and many other cryptocurrencies employ blockchain technology, in which every transaction is logged in a public ledger, creating chains of transactions. Computers linked in massive networks each have a copy of the ledger. Blockchain technology makes crypto-assets difficult to impossible to forge or manipulate, at least with the knowledge and computing power available today. Some commentators claim, though, that within just 20 years we will have machines powerful enough to crack all the encryption we currently use. But there are more immediate problems.

Many countries' financial supervisory authorities, such as Finansinspektionen in Sweden, have repeatedly warned of all the risks associated with cryptocurrencies – or crypto-assets, as some prefer to call them. The majority of these assets are not subject to regulation. They exist outside the established financial system and so lack any sort of consumer protection. While bitcoin and similar currencies were intended to be used as a means of payment, most purchasers have bought them primarily to speculate or as a store of value. So far, the new private digital currencies have not functioned as a means of payment on a major scale. That's why the world's central banks prefer the name crypto-asset to cryptocurrency.

Much of this experimentation out there in cyberspace is reminiscent of the events that took place in ancient China and the Middle East. Then as now, we solve practical problems that arise as society changes. As we know, some form of money is absolutely necessary for the functioning of complex societies. A standardised means of payment simplifies things, just as it did back then. And the great advantage of money is that you only need to keep track of the prices of things in terms of money, rather than an endless list of various barter exchanges.

But banknotes and coins have their downsides. Issuers have to use complicated printing and minting processes to guarantee authenticity. Users still have to rely on something in the physical world, with all that that entails. For example, coins and banknotes can be lost or stolen. They also take up space, and if we want to transfer them to someone else, we are dependent on a third party who can guarantee it will be done properly. That's often a bank that charges fees and might have views on where the money is sent. But, most importantly, notes and coins can lose some or all of their value if a bank goes bust or if too much money is created. Inflation – or, in extreme cases, hyperinflation. It's a well-known, recurring problem.

Cryptocurrencies. Bitcoin. Ethereum. Blockchains. Maybe they are the answer. But what is the question, really? This stuff about money, value and assets is getting stranger and harder to grasp.

'Curiouser and curiouser,' as Alice once said in her adventures in Wonderland.

How did we end up here? What rabbit hole did we fall into?

Alice in Wonderland followed the White Rabbit as he fretted, 'I'm late! I'm late for a very important date!' She followed him down a hole and descended mile after mile, before landing in a world where everything was unfamiliar. She could swim in a pool of her own tears. A caterpillar smoked a hookah, and a baby was transformed into a pig.

Alice had entered a very strange world, where things seemed to follow their own rules. Similarly, we, in the real world, followed Lord Byron's daughter Ada Lovelace into a world of numbers, dreams of an analytical machine and poetic science – a science in which intuition and imagination are just as important as mathematics and scientific concepts.

Ada Lovelace was a brilliant British mathematician, who is regarded as the creator of the first computer program. Back in the early 1840s, she developed a theoretical interest in steampunk versions of calculating machines. She and her colleague Charles Babbage called them 'analytical engines'. More than a century later, we started calling them computers. Without computers, there would be no cryptocurrencies. And crypto-currencies are probably the ultimate expression of the way computing power and new technologies have begun to revolutionise what we call money. Technological rabbit holes are nothing new. We fall into them all the time. Not all at the same time or in the same way. Nevertheless, there is a pattern. Technology is really just knowledge that has assumed a fixed form and has a best-before date. An iPhone is a small, neat package, filled with knowledge, with a best-before date that's often less than three years away – just like any can or jar. But the path towards an increasingly virtual economy started long before bitcoin. It's not just a question of technology.

People have always worshipped the abstract, regarding spiritual matters as superior to physical matters – purer, more rational. This principle has followed us through the history of religion and philosophy. Perhaps our high opinion of the spiritual has also contributed to developments in the economy? We have longed to get away from dirty manufacturing plants and crowded market squares to a clean, pleasant, weightless economy – no more coal-fired machinery and smoke-belching factories with grease stains on the floor.

The German philosopher Georg Wilhelm Friedrich Hegel theorised that history was suffused with a spirit that drove progress. There are three successive phases. First is the thesis, which is progress and maturation. It then crosses over into its own antithesis, a stage of over-maturity and internal contradiction. The final stage is synthesis, where the opposites are united in a higher state. Eventually, a new thesis emerges from the synthesis. Maybe old Hegel's spirit could help us understand, right now, just how things have turned out for our ape.

Today, we have two spirits driving historical progress. Information technology and financialisation have come to encompass every field of human endeavour. Two spirits dancing in the same space, taking turns, in a whirling waltz. Egging each other on. They both worship the spiritual, the weightless, the virtual. They also worship speed and performance. They don't want to be late for the future. As we will see, it is an audacious combination.

With the advent of computers, we set the first virtual spirit in motion: information technology. When new knowledge – new technology – comes along in a particular area, we use it first to improve, develop and stream-line what we already use. The first cars resembled horse-drawn carriages;

the horses had just been replaced by an engine. When the first commercial computers appeared, they were mainly used to perform the same tasks we had been doing already, only faster: archives, directories and accounting were some of those early uses. For the same reason, simple, self-contained money-management tasks were also computerised early on. The first automatic cash machine – also known as an ATM (short for automated teller machine) – was introduced in 1967 by Barclays Bank in the UK. This is an excellent illustration of the principle of a machine taking over a task people used to do: paying out cash, while making fewer mistakes and providing a faster service – after a while, anyway. For understandable reasons, most new technology has a few teething problems.

That's when it really opened up – the rabbit hole, that is. Things could get very 'curious' indeed. We started to use the new technology to do things we couldn't do before. Things that simply weren't possible. Now, cars can drive themselves and no longer look like horse-drawn carriages. A bookseller can find books you'll like – without asking you. When Amazon created a new kind of bookstore, with millions of titles, that became possible. Customers can easily find the book they're after in the vast store. That would have been impossible without machines able to search for and identify the right title among the millions of publications in stock.

New technology has contributed to the progress of trade throughout history. Sailing ships, carrier pigeons and telexes all helped us to exchange things more efficiently. The advent of computers and electronics turbocharged that progress. The basic principle is that anything that can be digitised will be digitised. Stock-market trading, which started on a bridge over the Damrak in 17th-century Amsterdam, went digital decades ago. Of course, banks' international transactions are handled electronically, and we do our banking on our phone or computer screen now. Nice and efficient, yet it's still something we recognise. These are all sophisticated modern versions of things we have been doing for a long time – trading, banking and money – all within the framework of nations and their laws.

Cryptocurrencies like bitcoin, on the other hand, are not regulated by any country. They are a new kind of money – a kind that can only come about far down a technological rabbit hole, in a place where nothing is recognisable. Cryptocurrencies differ from ordinary money, which originates either in an account as a claim on a private company (usually a bank) or as cash issued by a central bank – which would be a claim on a central bank's account. Perhaps cryptocurrencies are somewhat like the shells we used as a type of currency at the dawn of time. Like shells, they have absolutely no intrinsic value and are not backed by any nation state. That's something the world's central bankers often point out. They say that all dealings with cryptocurrencies are done at your own risk.

There are no countries at the bottom of the rabbit hole. No banks either. Cryptocurrencies exist alongside the established monetary system we have today. Crypto enthusiasts say it is precisely the involvement of governments, banks and people in our money that is the risk. They say they are finally creating a world where we can store and transfer value without sticky-fingered politicians and bank directors getting involved and generating uncertainty. In fact, many countries' central banks are already starting to worry what would happen if large numbers of people started to convert their assets into bitcoin or another cryptocurrency. That is the strange corner of reality where we find the competition between currencies that the cypherpunks want.

It is competition. While the world's geeks think about alternative currencies, we are making payments and money electronic in the old system. The tsunami of new tech that put a mobile phone in virtually every person's hand is already starting to eliminate banknotes and coins in some countries. As usual, Sweden is out in front. Dealing with cash is already something that would be classed as endangered if it were a plant or an animal. Without cash, and the ability to control the printing of cash, the Riksbank, Sweden's central bank, will lose control of the country's money. That's why Sweden is developing a digital form of the krona to replace coins and banknotes.

Of course, there are a lot of problems with cryptocurrencies today. They are still relatively complicated to use, a haven for illegal money, and mining (creating) cryptocurrencies requires vast amounts of electricity.

But, with a little imagination, they could also offer hope. Around half of all people in the world do not have a bank account. They are not bankable. In many cases, they do not have an ID card, assets or an address – all the things an old-fashioned banker asks for. But most of them do have a mobile phone – a computer, in other words. That gives the crypto world a way to open the door a crack to invite all the people of the world to join in and trade – not just things, but money as well.

Cryptocurrencies are part of a development sometimes referred to as financialisation: the second great spirit of our time. Bigger, better-functioning markets are firing up for everything, from money and shares to electricity and travel. Today, more and more profit in business comes directly and indirectly from trade with various financial instruments, rather than production of goods, or trading in goods. So, we are increasingly trading financial stuff. The business that started small, on a bridge over the Damrak in Amsterdam, as something of an exception, has become the norm. If we extend it with a more philosophical perspective, we could say that buying and selling on that bridge in Amsterdam was the start of a spiritualisation of the economy. Since then, the idea that we can buy and sell shares in economic activities has exploded all over the world. Our economies have changed. You could say that financialisation means our real economies have become virtual. Like a video game. 'Virtual' means that you create an artificial, simulated computer environment instead of the real world. The computer generates settings that seem real. Much of the economy happens in these virtual worlds and thus becomes more unreal.

Ever more ethereal and fluffy.

So, as the real economy becomes more financial, it becomes more virtual. At any rate, it feels that way for many of us who don't work in the world of finance every day. But, as we will see, it is still possible to understand what's going on. The financial part of the economy has expanded rapidly in recent decades – faster than the rest of the economy. The finance sector accounts for a larger share of the economy and now exercises greater influence over the way our economies function. We have gone from the situation a century ago – where physical assets were the most important production factor, the most important form of capital and the basis of value creation – to an economy where financial assets increasingly take that role.

In the Wild West of the American economy, the financial sector has tripled in size in four decades. It now makes up 7% of the US economy. But, even with all that capital, there is a snag deep down in capitalism. It used to be about saving some of what you've earned from your business and reinvesting it to make your business even better. Today, only a small proportion of American banks' lending goes on productive investments. The vast majority – 85% – goes on something else. And this 'something else' is buying and selling assets that already exist. It is done in the hope of buying something that will increase in value, which can then be sold at a profit. A house, a share or a bitcoin. Everything can and will be traded. Until the bubble bursts. And it will burst, as we have seen in the past and now.

It is often said that culture is all the things we humans do. Similarly, you could say that the economy is all the things we humans trade, and don't trade, with one another. Of course, the things we do and the things we trade with one another change over time. They are a reflection of our lives. Our trading of things says something about us. Whether we want it to or not, it makes our interests visible. Financialisation also says something. It says, for one thing, that we are living longer than ever. It's a story about our demographics. We need to set aside money somehow for the long period when we won't be working: our pension. This is where the financial spirit is really picking up the pace.

Aside from billions of people's personal savings for old age and the future, the spirit of financialisation was fuelled by the transformation of pension systems in social-welfare states. We can look at the Netherlands and Sweden as examples. Previously, the pension systems in both countries had been based on a structure with major state involvement – a commitment by the state that there was money earmarked for your old age. For a while, that gave citizens a feeling of security. But the state pension obligations also built up enormous mountains of debt, particularly as demographic shifts meant an ageing population. Something needed to be done to secure future pensions, so the system was reformed to permit pension contributions to be invested in the stock market. Citizens were also given opportunities to invest directly or indirectly in shares or investment funds.

In the Netherlands, trade unions had a great deal of influence over the pension system. They sensed opportunities in investing in the stock market. Stocks seemed to generate much larger dividends than old-fashioned, low-risk bond yields. And the traditional types of pension arrangements were finding it more difficult to cover their obligations because of increasing lifespans. The change suited the state as well, because it lightened the state's obligations. Naturally, employers were also pleased. They didn't need to contribute as much if investments generated good returns. So everybody was happy. But our friends in the financial market were probably happiest of all. Vast amounts of pension capital were flooding into the world's stock markets.

Of course, not everyone chose exactly the same route as the Netherlands. Different countries have their own systems. But the general direction and principles have been the same. Investing citizens' pensions in the stock market gave the best returns, for a reasonable risk. So, instead of purchasing interest-bearing government bonds that generate a low but highly reliable yield, pension administrators started investing more in stock markets around the world. In a climate with interest rates near zero, that seemed like an obvious move. Citizens were also encouraged to use the stock market to save for their retirement. In the case of Sweden, a special publicly administered system was set up, creating a fund market with individual 'premium pension savings.' Individuals could decide for themselves how that part of their pension savings would be invested. The message was that, with a little effort, everyone could add that special little 'extra' to their retirement. Higher risk, but also higher returns – over time, at any rate. And on average. But, as the small print says whenever you invest in shares and funds: 'Past performance is no guarantee of future results.'

Whatever your own view, pension reforms have pumped vast amounts of savings capital into the stock market. For most people, though, saving money has become so complex that many prefer to let a specialist handle

it: a bank, or perhaps a fund manager. You might pick out a few funds and
then let them manage the rest. They administer things virtually. Many
of us lack 'financial literacy.' The financial segment of the economy is
increasingly abstract and incomprehensible for the average person. And,
just as with every other area where most of us lack expertise – the law,
medicine or architecture, for example – specialised professions arise to
help out. Usually for a fee.

Maybe things started to get difficult with the first 'derivative,' several
hundred years ago. You may remember the options that were invented
during the Dutch East India Company's trading voyages to Java, when
nervous and optimistic Amsterdam merchants started buying and selling shares in various voyages. Then they invented derivatives – that is,
the right to buy or sell a share in the future at a certain price, at a certain
time or during a certain period. That sort of trading was a relatively
marginal practice for a long time. Today, though, derivatives trading
is anything but marginal. The value of the derivatives market in 2006,
not long before the big financial crisis, was $1.2 quadrillion. The same
year, global GDP was $50 trillion. Numbers of that magnitude are hard
to comprehend, but it's the relative amounts we're interested in. And
we can see that, in the 21st century, the world's total GDP is marginal
in relation to derivatives.

In finance, the term 'derivatives' refers to a whole group of different
instruments: options, futures, warrants and variants thereof – each word
more mystifying than the last. But they all share one familiar feature: they
enable investors to take a risk or avoid a risk in exchange for payment.
Optimists and pessimists can trade with each other. Just as in our little
story about the Dutch East Indies traders who later founded a company,
there are always some people who cannot, are unable to or do not want
to wait and see how things turn out in the future.

'Derivative' means that something is based on something else. There is
an underlying basis for these sorts of securities. They derive their value
from something else. They are like mirrors reflecting a different reality,
mirrors that sharpen and enlarge reality.

And this is where things start to get virtual – without a computer in sight. It's like a funhouse chamber of mirrors around everything. Often, the underlying asset is a share, or a share index, but it might also be a currency or a commodity. Or something else entirely. Electricity, for example. The point is that you are not trading in the share or currency directly. Instead, you are speculating about its value – not today, but at some point in the future.

And this is where things get more virtual.

You are simply betting that something will happen in the future. That sounds like something people would do for fun, but it's actually highly practical.

Buying and selling derivatives is a way of protecting yourself, to avoid a risk, or to purposefully take a risk. A simple example is if someone wants to protect themselves and avoid a foreign-exchange risk. Currency exchange rates fluctuate all the time. Let's say you want to sell something for $1,000 in the future – say, six months from now – and you want to be certain that the dollars you receive will be worth exactly a certain amount in kronor. You can purchase a future, which will commit both you and the seller to a certain exchange rate on a certain date in the future. Now you have paid a sum of money to eliminate the risk that your $1,000 won't be worth a certain amount in kronor in the future. Some types of derivatives actually allow you to buy and sell risks. In our example above, someone takes the risk, for a fee, that the dollars I receive six months from now will be worth less in kronor than today. Nice and practical for someone who deals in a lot of currencies and wants to sleep well at night.

But there are many kinds of risk. So there are many ways of dealing with risk. An option is the same as a future in the example above, but with two important differences. A future is an agreement today, but payment and delivery must take place on the agreed date. An option is optional for the purchaser. You have the right to buy or sell a particular item for a particular price, up until a particular date. So there is no risk that the price will change. You can exercise your option at any time from today, whenever you want, from the date of the agreement until the end date. A warranty is a long option – a year or longer. It gives you the right to buy or sell underlying value at a particular price. You pay a premium for that right. Here, too, the idea is to avoid a risk in exchange for payment. Or, on the contrary, to assume a risk in exchange for payment. The world is full of risks. There is always a mix of optimists and pessimists. And so there is a whole little ecosystem of derivatives in every imaginable flavour. Some are used mainly to protect against risk, others to speculate with risk. Derivatives can generate enormous gains – and enormous losses – in your invested capital. That's something we explained earlier, but it bears repeating.

So, nearly everything can be bought and sold, now that we have that made-up stuff called money. Even risk. As we found earlier, that's what's magical about money. Anything can be exchanged for anything else via money. Ultimately, the only limits on what we can trade are set by our morals, laws and our imagination. Certain things are easier to buy and sell than others, of course. The easiest things are the sort of items that are fairly standardised, where both the buyer and seller know what they are dealing with. Currencies, securities and commodities like wheat, copper or oil are traded round the clock. But even goods like certain kinds of wine, or services like shipping and production capacity can be defined and parcelled into standard units to be bought and sold on the market. And – hey presto – the whole mechanism of buying and selling risk can start up. Goods and services go from being assets to being liquid assets. That means they can be sold immediately   transformed into money. You can think of goods and services as 'frozen' money, which the market thaws out and turns to liquid. In the 21st century, we seem to be capable of getting most things to flow like water.

It's when the financialisation spirit gets together with information technology that things really get going. Then our two dancing spirits really pick up the tempo. More and bigger markets are linked together in a globe-spanning network – virtual marketplaces, with much of the world taking part. Exchanging things – as well as risks – can now take on astronomical proportions.

In Silicon Valley, sometimes called the Rome of our era, we often find the most extreme ways of utilising contemporary markets. And it's no wonder. Perhaps more than anywhere else on Earth, this is where we encounter present-day explorers. But they are not travelling across the seven seas like the Dutch and Portuguese, trying to discover the world. They are using technology to build entirely new worlds. High-tech explorers travelling through time, with grand ambitions, taking huge risks. But, just as in the age of the great explorers, pots of gold await those who are first. Today, there is a tradition of working with what has come to be called venture capital. The name gives some indication of what we're talking about: namely, special investment firms that invest huge sums of capital in entrepreneurs' new ventures, or companies, and take on some risk to accelerate their progress. Venture capital is a way of pouring petrol on a little economic fire, or injecting anabolic steroids into the dancers' legs, if we're thinking about our spirits. Making things go fast. The first one to reach the future gets a pot of gold.

As you will notice, the concept of venture capital has certain parallels with derivatives. It's about investing in the future. Of course, all businesses are doing this, but the future often carries a special importance for pioneering Silicon Valley companies. It also worships speed, rapid expansion. The first-mover advantage. They love their industry jargon in Silicon Valley. The first one to make a move and commandeer a future market gains an advantage. Maybe you could think of it as a sort of colonisation of the future. The first company to come along can acquire a dominant position – something the old Austrian economist and communist opponent Joseph Schumpeter so accurately dubbed a temporary monopoly. Then, these companies form the platform. They become the market. That's exactly what Google, Facebook and many others have done. Several of them have temporary virtual monopolies in their markets today – to the delight of their owners and to the horror of the world's anti-competition authorities.

Potential future profits can be – and often are – huge. That is often a feature of a monopoly. That's why it is less important whether a company earns any money today. You can sacrifice a bit today to get pots of gold tomorrow. It's the future that counts. This explains why venture-capital firms pour millions, and sometimes billions of dollars into relatively new companies that make losses for many years. If their business concept seems good enough, there will always be someone willing to take the risk and purchase shares.

We can also find the principle of being quick to colonise the future outside of Silicon Valley. The financial craft developed in the suburbs of San Francisco has gained adherents all over the world – particularly in the Nordic countries. Spotify, the Swedish music-streaming company founded in 2006, is just one of many examples. It has expanded and expanded to become the world's biggest online music service. But it did not actually show a profit until 2021 – 15 years after the company was founded. Along the way, Spotify's founders became some of the richest people in Sweden and the world, despite the company's losses. First and biggest. Following the Silicon Valley model. A temporary monopoly in streaming music, in the world. Now, they just have to bring home their pots of gold.

Wild, risky, ridiculous – you might think so. Yet it's also entirely understandable, and something familiar from the bridges of Amsterdam. You remember. That ape – who is us – just wanted something tasty to eat. Back then, the aromas of exotic spices prompted some of us to take huge risks and invent new ways to create and own businesses. Now, the same ape wants to listen to nice things. Music. And, in fact, it's the same tune here and now, in our fancy modern world, as 400 years ago: big risks and a few new ways of starting companies   all to make things tasty, comfortable and pleasant for the ape that is us.

The super-entrepreneur Elon Musk and his Tesla electric-car company may well be the most famous example in the 2020s of just how wild things can get in the hunt for a temporary monopoly, pots of gold and territory in the future transport industry. He became the world's richest person by selling electric vehicles, but he made a loss for two whole decades! He founded Tesla in 2003, launched the first car model in 2008, and the company made its first profit in 2021. And, yes, its head office until 2021 was in none other than Palo Alto, in the heart of California's Silicon Valley. Tesla is a car company structured like a high-tech company. Over the same two decades, houses in Detroit, the capital of the old car industry, were literally falling to pieces.

Losses for nearly 20 years – that takes stamina and a somewhat different way of viewing companies and how they are built up. Investments in the finance world are often relatively short-term. Significantly shorter than 20 years. In the venture-capital sector, people often figure on an investment horizon of six to seven years. How does that work? Investors often specialise in a certain phase of a company's life. Some are particularly keen on new start-ups; others focus on start-ups that have made some progress and have a bit of a track record. You go in, work to achieve rapid expansion and growth for a period of time, and then you get out. Then other investors come in with the knowledge and experience needed for the next step. It's a sort of relay, with different investors taking a brand-new start-up to a launch on the stock market. Ideally, all the way to unicorn status – that's the term for a company worth more than a billion dollars.

But how is anyone supposed to navigate this curious Alice in Wonderland world, with cryptocurrencies and unicorns trying to colonise the future? The finance market and tech industry are waltzing around at an ever-increasing tempo. All the world's pension funds, eager for returns, are egging them on. In fact, it may all seem and feel more complicated than it really is. New jargon and abbreviations, together with speed and huge numbers, may obscure our vision. Perhaps it's not that complicated, if you really think about it.

We must remember that our exchanging of things – everything we do in an economy – is just a reflection of our lives. And our lives still begin and end in nature. Sometimes our trading is a funhouse mirror that twists and distorts reality, but it is still a mirror. The expansion of the virtual economy has a tendency to end up in data centres – that's how virtual the economy is. Just think about Amazon, planning to build data centres in the Swedish town of Eskilstuna. Or Facebook's data centre in Luleå, in Sweden's far north. These are vast facilities that each gobble up as much energy as a city the size of Uppsala, with some 200,000 residents. The computing cloud is neither soft, fluffy nor weightless. It actually consists of huge rectangular hunks of steel and precious metals – which consume a whole lot of electricity. And obscure the view. Bitcoin and other cryptocurrencies have similar effects. Encryption requires vast amounts of computing power. In fact, cryptocurrency companies have even bought decommissioned coal-fired power stations and started them up again. All to get energy for their weightless currency.

So, where is all this leading us? Well, to the realisation that the virtual world is just a simulation of reality. It's not a different reality, just an image. Behind the image, we still have the same planet and the same reality ticking along. At the end of the day, bitcoin – the rock star – and all its grandchildren are a modern variation on the shells we experimented with as methods of payment at the dawn of history. Private inventions to make exchanging things easier, which have now entered a computer-simulated world. Silicon Valley is the Amsterdam of our age, our voyage of discovery, bringing adventure, huge risks and extreme success, all packaged and fuelled by men and women who come up with ever more sophisticated ways to share risk and trade in risk. Just like on the bridge over the Damrak. Sure, things are a lot faster now. And, yes, so many more people are involved today. The capital base is also so much bigger. But finance, transactions and trading is still just a reflection. At the bottom of today's technological rabbit hole, we find the same thing: ourselves.

The same natural world that chirps and caws.

The same ape that wants tasty things to eat and drink.

And good music to dance to.

Maybe it's time for all of us to take that red pill mentioned in the Wachowskis' cult film *The Matrix*. The one that makes people see reality for what it really is, not what it appears to be. With a red pill inside us, we see that a new spirit is inviting us to dance. The ape's eternal dance partner. An old acquaintance that is now going to set the agenda for our lives. Again.

Nature.

UPROAR IN THE GLOBAL VILLAGE

In which the ape manages
to open and close
a fast-food restaurant,
and the Empire
strikes back.

Sometimes the phenomenon is referred to as an oxymoron.

Most people have experienced the sensation of wanting or feeling two things at the same time. Social psychologists call this *cognitive dissonance*.

Dilemmas and unresolvable conflicts exist in our own little lives and in the wider world. In fact, we are surrounded by them. In our own lives, we want to belong to a group. But we also want freedom. If we blast off into orbit like a satellite and observe the *whole* world, we can find similar dilemmas on a larger scale. The most obvious one is perhaps the clash between local life, here, in our little corner, and what has come to be called the *global situation*. In more and more areas, our life is interconnected, as if there were no borders. The Internet is a vast nervous system that encompasses our globe. Multinational corporations, led by Coca-Cola and CNN, see the *whole* world as their market. Half of all commerce today is linked, either directly or indirectly, to the world's multinational corporations.

It's easy to understand why companies and businesspeople circle the globe like commercial spirits. It's their job to find new things, just like Vasco da Gama, Columbus or any other explorer. In early 2020, a little virus made it obvious just how dependent we are on one another in a globalised economy. International supply chains were severed when borders were closed. Production of everything from computers to dishwashers was interrupted. Then, two years later, when bombs started to rain over Ukraine, the world's pantries felt the impact. Ukraine and Russia are two agricultural giants, with customers all over the world.

It's true that we trade with one another as if borders didn't exist. But we also talk and play with one another the same way. It's difficult to find a part of the world – in terms of geography or activity – that has not been caught up in the international web. If we look around, it's remarkable, to say the least, to see how intertwined our lives have become. Scientists share knowledge as easily as if they were all in the same building. Performers write songs that are played worldwide. Sports stars are traded on the global market like any other product. And exclusion from the global playground and marketplace has been transformed into a powerful weapon. Just look at the way much of the world chose to respond to Russia's invasion of Ukraine in early spring of 2022: sanctions and isolation.

Not everyone chose to cut Russia off, though. The two most populous nations – India and the People's Republic of China – refuse to take a clear stand against Russia. South Africa and a number of other countries have chosen the same stance. Clearly, there is a competing mindset. The dream of the global village has started to crumble.

How do sanctions work? How do you exclude someone from the marketplace? The ape inside us wants to be part of the group. Ostracism, or banishing someone, was regarded as a severe punishment in Ancient Greece, where the word originated. For the moment, let's ignore those few people who choose to isolate themselves, and a Russia that is closing itself off. People in general want to feel they belong. Places and groups have always been important to us: local issues; the clan; a village, a country or a continent. But, in the 21st century, we are in a state of flux. We seem to be realigning which people, places and things we identify with. Our lives are becoming an oxymoron – a round square – as our small, local lives are now blended with large-scale events. Whether we like it or not, technology is smashing down borders, with smartphones making a particular impact – or starting to, anyway. As we will see, the same technologies can also be used to exclude and isolate.

We have always been on the move. We have a fundamental urge to explore the world around us. That's how we eventually managed to conquer it. Today, people live everywhere it's possible to settle and create a tolerable life. European explorers like Vasco da Gama and Chinese seafarers like Zheng He – and many more – regarded it as their life's mission to unlock the secrets of the world. Centuries later, in 1986, Harvard professor Michael Porter would dub our zeal for conquering the world 'globalisation.' The latter half of the 1900s saw international attitudes and activities quickly moving from being the exception to the rule. The 1970s saw the start of growth in global trade, international investment and travel. Growth in those sectors really exploded in the 1980s.

It's easy to look back and understand what happened – that's usually the case. Businessmen and companies the world over have always sought out new markets. They are commercial explorers, in a way, always on the hunt for something that can make their business bigger and better. After two horrific world wars, the world opened up – slowly at first, but then, by the 1970s, new technologies had stepped up the pace.

That was when middle-class lifestyles started to conquer the Western world. The idea of free trade tore down one toll barrier after another. In the 1950s, the first chartered plane of Swedish tourists touched down on Mallorca (after four stops along the way). Little pieces of plastic called *credit cards* came into use as means of payment. In the mid-1980s, a gap opened up in the world. The Middle Kingdom, the mysterious closed People's Republic of China – with a population of over a billion – cautiously opened its doors to the rest of the world. Less than a decade later, the Soviet Union's communist empire imploded. Cheap mobile phones and the World Wide Web fuelled progress. At the dawn of the 21st century, a patchwork of nations and borders had become a global playground.

Today, most companies are born as global citizens. Spotify, the music-streaming site born in Sweden, had a presence in 20 countries before its seventh birthday. Facebook conquered much of the world in just a few years. Companies are often the source of new developments. They drive change and innovation – and that's no surprise. If you're subject to constant competition, you'll become innovative. Inventiveness is crucial for survival. In their never-ending quest to get better at what they do and find bigger markets and even more amazing talents, companies venture out into the world. And then the rest of us follow. We are pulled along. Today, it's actually hard to find a single human activity that hasn't been sucked into the international slipstream, either directly or indirectly.

Things that used to be exotic and exceptional are now the norm in the 2020s. At least, that's how it looked.

Maybe that era has also come to an end, nothing more than a shiny golden arch extending across three decades or so, promising everyone a place at the table at the big globalisation party. Or, in more figurative terms, *two* golden arches. McDonald's opened its first restaurant in Moscow's Red Square on 31 January 1990, just as the party was getting started. It was an event rich in symbolism. Russians stood in long snaking queues for a chance to taste the new world that awaited them, a world they had long thought existed far away in the West, but had never had a chance to experience. Thirty-two years later, in the spring of 2022, a man was interviewed as he queued to order hamburgers at McDonald's in Moscow. It was the last day before the branch closed in protest at Russia's brutal invasion of Ukraine. The man's father had stood in line on that first day in 1990. Now, he was there on the last day.

Ever since the fall of the Berlin Wall, the European Union (EU) has pursued a trade policy towards authoritarian and totalitarian states like China and Russia that is described by the German phrase *Wandel durch Handel*, which means 'transformation through trade.' Trade promotes dialogue and cooperation. Eventually, mutual economic interdependency will make military conflict impossible, or at least so undesirable that it ceases to be a real threat. Trade and the market economy, with all their dialogue and free exchange of information, will be the 'soft power' that also helps to spread democracy. Democratic ideals come along as a bonus. Products and pop culture create a mutual interdependency among countries. The more, the better, and it also promotes democracy. So the thinking went, at any rate.

And that wasn't surprising. The EU was founded on those ideas. Its cooperation is the best example we have that it actually works. Germany and France, two countries whose conflicts contributed to two world wars, have lived together in peace since then. The European Coal and Steel Union, formed shortly after the Second World War, is regarded as the first step towards today's EU.

Against that background, it's easy to see why EU member states –

particularly reunited Germany, the engine driving the EU's economy –
advocated that policy. *Wandel durch Handel* was exemplified by events
like Angela Merkel's unflappable discussions with Vladimir Putin.
She spoke both German and Russian, having grown up in communist
East Germany. He spoke both Russian and German, after his years
in East Germany as a KGB agent. And those discussions led to the
construction of natural-gas pipelines between Russia and Germany.
First one pipeline, and then another one. Trade and dialogue, mutual
interdependence, with a former German chancellor on the board of
the gas company.

We all simply want the best. The Russians, too. And the Chinese.
Everybody does. Vaccines or wines – the principle is the same. And it's
perfectly reasonable that students seek out the cheapest beer and the
best universities. When Microsoft or Volvo are looking for new talent,
of course they want the best candidates. And why watch some local TV
series when Tom Cruise and his *Top Gun: Maverick* mega-production is
just a few presses of the button away? The principle is simple. We want
the best we can get. And that goes for everything. Or so we thought.

If you're invited to the party and get to see an open, democratic, liberal
society, that ought to be irresistible. Right?

But a bitter truth has emerged: all the meetings with Putin and all
the Western companies investing in Russia have clearly not ensured any
democratic progress there. Nor has all the trade with China changed the
political situation there. Quite the opposite. In the early 21st century, the
1990s movement towards increasing openness and democratic influence
came to a halt and started to go in reverse, even though China's economy
was booming and its trade with the West continued to set new records.
Instead, China's president Xi Jinping tightened the thumbscrews on
Chinese society. Freedom of expression started to wither. China's Internet was placed behind a firewall – a digital Great Wall of China. Once
again, walls were being built instead of ships. Sports stars, pop stars and
oligarchs were muzzled.

Wandel durch Handel.

Boom.

One night, in February 2022, Russian president Vladimir Putin rolled his tanks into neighbouring Ukraine.

A major war. Bombs and missiles in the middle of the global village. Millions of refugees, along with reports of thousands of deaths, dominated the news channels. A few weeks later, much of the world had formulated its answer: Russia was to be isolated as much as possible – cut off from the global party.

Cutting Russia off turned out to be easier said than done. Europe is tied to Russian gas production through its pipelines. Sanctions drove up global market prices for oil and gas, which actually *increased* Russia's oil and gas revenues in the short term. The economy was playing a trick on us. Supply and demand. A reduction in supply drove up the price of Russian natural gas, which the EU was then obligated to purchase.

Reduced access to many commodities – not just natural gas, but also oil, wheat, maize and fertiliser – and continued shortages of semiconductors and precious metals for electronics meant that another familiar word made an unexpected comeback in the global economy and our household budgets: namely, inflation. A ten-year period of practically no inflation is over. While Sweden's Riksbank and other central banks had an annual inflation target of 2%, the actual inflation rate was often even lower. Meanwhile, interest rates were near zero – or even negative. Not a normal situation.

Inflation means increasing prices. In traditional economic theory, it is regarded as good to have some inflation, but the rate should be lower than economic growth. *Deflation* refers to the opposite, when prices decrease. That is undesirable. There is also *stagflation*, which refers to a combination of *inflation* and economic *stagnation*, or an absence of growth. Many countries experienced stagflation during the 1970s oil crisis. That economic crisis was also caused by a war – in that case, in the Middle East. The world wants to avoid another dose of stagflation. But inflation is definitely back, and it needs to be dealt with.

The traditional way for central banks to counteract inflation is by raising interest rates, which makes it more expensive to borrow money. Then there is less money for consumption and it becomes more expensive to invest. The idea is that higher interest rates will cause demand to shrink, which will reduce pressure on prices. This method obviously works best when inflation is actually driven by excessive consumption, or *demand*. If the problem is caused by bottlenecks in *supply*, or production – in the form of war or pandemic, for example – then it is less certain that raising interest rates will solve the problem. Higher interest rates don't solve the problem of production capacity. Instead, they make investing in higher production capacity more expensive.

Globalisation and lower interest rates have meant a long period of increasing supply, fewer bottlenecks and big pressure on prices. Chinese workers employed on the 'world's factory floor' producing all the things that filled the world's shops had low wage requirements, in global terms. If their wage demands rose, more workers soon came in from rural China. When the supply of cheap Chinese labour started to run out, some production moved to Vietnam. And then to another low-wage country. Combined with a more streamlined logistics chain and complex division of labour, globalisation overall led to low inflationary pressure. That has now changed once again. Bam.

First, a virus. Then, a war. Suddenly, open borders are not a given.

In different ways, the first pandemic of the 21st century, war in Ukraine and subsequent sanctions have highlighted the strengths and weaknesses in our internationally networked economy. Thanks to new technology and online solutions, we could mitigate some of the pandemic's impacts as we shut down our societies. Nice and robust, with plenty of bandwidth and smartphones in many people's hands, some jobs and industries were hardly affected. But not everything is digital, weightless and knowledge-based. Not even the cloud. Acts of aggression, including shooting and shelling, have had a real effect. Ukraine's digitalised national library and the Ukrainian government's public documents had to be saved by Swedish archivists, donating their free time to make new backup copies. The electronic documents were stored in the *cloud*. But this particular cloud was on the ground, on servers dotted around Ukraine. Servers in danger of being blown to smithereens, which would cause the cloud to go up in smoke. Real smoke, not just digital.

The war has also reminded us that Ukraine and Russia are two of the world's leading exporters of wheat and maize. Together, they represent 30% of global wheat exports and 20% of maize exports. Some countries are almost wholly dependent on Ukraine and Russia for wheat – large countries, with hundreds of millions of people, including Egypt, Tunisia and parts of Turkey. In East Africa, 90% of the wheat consumed comes from Ukraine and Russia. But that's not all. If people in particularly vulnerable countries suffer from hunger as a result of rising wheat prices, they may be able to obtain help from the United Nations World Food Programme.

That's a good thing. But, in a globalised world, everything is inter-connected.

The UN World Food Programme usually purchased around half its wheat from – you guessed it – Ukraine. But, when missiles are raining down, Ukraine can no longer grow as much wheat as usual, much less export it.

We are back among the economy's fundamental driving forces. Baking bread. The ape that wants tasty things to eat. Wheat growing in fields that are ploughed much as they were back in Kushim the bookkeeper's day. Now wheat is exported from Ukraine to Egypt, rather than being grown in Mesopotamia. But the roots are the same.

We have the same needs.

We need food, and we need our health. We are still basically the same apes. The globalised world has given us some bumper years, but it has also made us very dependent on one another. On good cooperation. On things working without any hitches – with complete trust.

Trust increased to the extent that we no longer thought we needed any inventories in reserve.

We just had to place an order if we needed more.

Slightly smaller inventories meant slightly larger profit margins.

So we chose slightly smaller inventories.

And things got slightly cheaper.

But two years spent with a virulent virus highlighted the weakest links in the global supply chain – the same brutal lesson the war in Ukraine would teach us again. Shortages of everything from face masks to microchips and industrial components exposed the risks of purchasing things from a distant country specialising in that particular item.

We were already familiar with the advantages of that way of doing things. We had forgotten about the disadvantages. Suddenly, geography and our own countries were of crucial importance. Again. At first glance, it might look like a major resurgence for the 200-odd countries of the world – for now, anyway. But many of our biggest current problems and challenges really *are* transnational and require cooperation. We also know from the world of commerce that bigger markets are better than small ones. Maybe that's why something is taking shape on the horizon with echoes of former empires: a world in which countries are grouped together, willingly or unwillingly, under a political umbrella, distancing themselves from the rest of the world. The crystal ball is shrouded in darkness when we try to see whether the world will break up into three, five or seven empires.

Of course, the world's future political divisions will impact our economy. The way we do business – or exchange things, as we express it in this book – will change. The game plan will be somewhat reminiscent of the bad old days when the USA and the USSR each dominated their half of the world. The Cold War, as it was often called. We can still sense echoes of that era, as well as the old colonial empires. When the members of the United Nations voted to condemn Russia after its invasion of Ukraine, some democratic countries, including South Africa and Namibia, abstained from the vote rather than vote against Russia. That was not much of a surprise. That voting pattern could be seen as a rapid initial prognosis of the current strategic realignment. Who is loyal to whom? The recruitment campaign for the new empires has begun.

Some old ties to Russia have remained intact since the Soviet era, echoes of the times when the Soviets supported African liberation movements. Cuban soldiers used to be stationed in places like Angola to support the battle against Portuguese colonial control. Many guerrilla leaders – who would later become political leaders – were educated at Soviet universities.

Further echoes come from Russian arms exports. Even today, a number of countries are linked to the Russian empire via these economic and political ties. India is the largest in terms of area and population. India is a democracy, but it buys more than half its arms from Russia. Does this mean India is moving towards becoming part of a Russian economic empire? Presumably not. What about the other way round? Perhaps Russia might become part of India's sphere of interest? The subcontinent has a population ten times that of Russia. At the time of writing, Russia and India are in talks to set up a new payment system to replace SWIFT. Payment routes could be one way of redrafting the borders of new economic empires: the Western SWIFT empire; the Eastern (Chinese) Unipay empire. These flows of money bind nations together like threads. Politics and economics. Economics and politics.

But, beyond certain similarities to previous eras, we know nothing about what will happen next – as usual. Like the former empires, the new ones will probably argue and compete for allies and access to resources – natural resources, in particular. Despite all our advances, we have seen that everything starts and ends with nature. And, like their predecessors, the new empires will make claims about their own superiority. They will want to attract and retrain skilled people – now, even more than before. We will likely face extreme challenges. There are so many more people now, and our technology is so much more powerful.

But how will we – how must we – navigate in this (not so) brave new world of jittery empires, constant squalls and unanticipated storm clouds? It's a question we can always ask. Every day, in fact. We have always been intrigued by what the future holds, even if our predictions are usually little more than qualified guesses. It's so hard to investigate something that doesn't exist yet. And, as we know, the future isn't here yet.

The world's economic elites (and some political elites as well) get together every year in Davos, high on a Swiss mountain peak, to discuss the state of the world, at the World Economic Forum. To try to gaze at the present and the future. Maybe the crisp Alpine air helps to sharpen their ideas. One crucial, frequently recurring question in recent years up there on the mountain and among the world's economists in academia is whether economic growth can continue in the same way as it has over the past century. And, as so often happens when we are faced with a choice between paths, there are two distinct perspectives: on the one hand, weighty arguments for the feasibility of continued growth; on the other, a solid basis for arguing against growth in principle. At the risk of oversimplifying things, you could say it's a matter of deciding whether to press on the gas pedal or the brake. The question may appear easy, but the answers are difficult.

If we follow the neoclassical economists and view the economy as (largely) disconnected from nature, then a rocketing rate of economic growth could be fine. The economy could continue to grow sevenfold – or more – each century. Between 1900 and 2018, the world's population increased fivefold, GDP per capita increased sevenfold, and the total size of the global economy increased by a factor of 35. For example, little Sweden moved several rungs up the ladder in just over a century. We went from being one of the poorest countries in Europe in the mid-19th century to one of the world's richest nations by around 1970. Since then, we have been a permanent fixture in the global top ten. *No problemo.* Well, actually, there were a few problems, but, compared to the gains Sweden made in prosperity, lifespan and other metrics, the problems seemed small at the time.

Clearly, we are inventive. Let's keep inventing and creating new things. In this picture, economic growth is a function of labour, capital and human innovation, which continuously increases productivity. We are constantly coming up with smarter ways to produce, and we constantly get a little more out of what we put in. And we solve problems along the way. Just look at how we managed to tame humanity's three evil companions: war, famine and plague. They used to be there, always alongside us. But today, microbes, food shortages and unrest are no longer unfathomable disasters. They have been transformed into fully comprehensible problems, where we often – though certainly not always – manage to take control of the situation.

The sky's the limit! as they say.

However, if we see a link between economic growth and consumption of the planet's resources, as well as production of waste and pollution, then things get a little trickier. We need to step on the brakes. If 'the sky's the limit,' then that indicates that the sky – and what happens there – actually *has* a limit. Carbon dioxide emissions into the atmosphere are one of the factors that limit us.

The argument in favour of reining in growth is about a fundamentally different view of what the economy is and what it is not – particularly the role of energy and materials. We need to extend the boundaries of what is included in economic thinking and decision-making. They have to be placed in a larger context. Sometimes, scientists from other disciplines get annoyed at economists and say they suffer from physicist envy, because they wish they had an exact science. That's why economists like to use strange formulas – to make them appear more scientific, more like physics, the queen of all sciences. Well, maybe physics is now on the way to becoming part of economics. Bear with me on this, and you will soon understand why. Buckle up. This is pure physics. Or economics.

The ecological view of economic growth says that all resources in the economy come from nature, in one way or another. Those fixed resources may be renewable organic resources, or non-renewable, such as minerals. Resources return to nature in the form of products, emissions or waste. Sooner or later, they are emitted into the environment, the atmosphere, seas and lakes. Every physicist is familiar with the law of thermodynamics, which says that all material seeks its lowest potential energy state. Larger molecules are broken down into smaller ones. And smaller. Expressed in everyday language, it means that, over time, everything – absolutely everything – becomes worm food.

Even us, unfortunately. That's physics.

We can say that the material part of the economy, or the world, is a closed system – finite. There is a fixed quantity of materials. It does not grow or shrink; it just changes form. The planet Earth determines the system's outer limit: the limit of the economic-ecological system. The good news is that nature is constantly renewing everything that can be renewed. It loops, causes things to grow back, again and again. And change form, again and again. A virtuous circle, no doubt about it.

That also means there is no *production* in the economy, and no *consumption* – just *transformation*. The material just changes form, from an unusable form to a usable one. That's what we usually call production. Then it goes back to an unusable form. That's what we usually call consumption.

But perhaps the key insight with regard to economic theory, and therefore economic practice, is that economic processes are not abstract zeros and ones, but chemical, biological and physical processes. Always. Therefore, they can have absolute limits and obey certain laws of physics. Above all, economic processes cannot be permitted to exceed planetary limits in the long term. According to this view, there are certain limits which economic growth must remain within. The planet is a closed system, with fixed resources. That's logical and comprehensible.

So, we're left with the resources we've got. There's just one thing that keeps being added to the system from outside, that runs it: namely, energy from the sun.

Cosmic.

Or natural.

Our ape feels right at home. Things are growing and sprouting from the ground. There are figs and nuts available for picking. Wheat is ripening in the fields. The sun is shining.

Sunlight triggers photosynthesis in plants and bacteria, transforming carbon dioxide into oxygen and sugar. Warmth from the sun triggers wind, rain and tides, which become kinetic energy in our power stations. We gain motion and energy flows in addition to material. And growing biomass. The question is: is this enough to generate continuous, eternal economic growth?

One group of environmental economists believes it is not. They advocate something they call *degrowth*. Downsizing. They say that economic growth, the eternal expansion of the economy, needs to stop. Size itself is a problem. The more economic activity, the more natural resources are consumed, they say. And there is a direct link between

GDP and our material footprint – a linear relationship. If growth tends towards infinity, we will eventually exceed the Earth's limits.

If the size of the economy is instead scaled down, then our emissions and our material footprint will decrease. Put very simply, these economists are making the point that economic growth per se does not make us happier, because GDP is a blunt instrument that ignores a host of factors, such as all the negative effects on the ecosystems we are a part of. Thus, there is no reason to strive for continuous growth. Instead, we should achieve a good society by other means, focusing on the goal – prosperity – instead of economic growth. Can the idea of growth, that everyone gets *more*, be replaced with the idea of improvement, that we get the same amount, but, in exchange, our *well-being* improves?

Another group of environmental economists believes that it is still possible to achieve eternal economic growth. They say it is wishful thinking to believe that we can reorganise the entire global economy and the political system in every country in the way advocated by degrowth economists, and do it before it's too late to stop climate change. Furthermore, a shrinking economy lacks funding for all the investment in green technology that will be needed. The best chance we have, according to this second group – which could be termed *green growth* – is massive investment and rapid adoption of green tech. In this model, conversion to green energy itself drives growth.

Of course, it is far from certain that this can and will work. But the degrowth scenario does not seem entirely convincing either. Downsizing, or at least reducing economic growth, is an extremely tough political sell. Even the name *degrowth* seems psychologically unappealing. It makes it sound as if we'll all get poorer, having less and less: a tough idea to sell. The ape likes it when things grow and flourish. The ape likes more, not less. It is usually difficult to take things away from us when we're accustomed to having them. Especially hope.

There is plenty of room here to rethink things on a big scale. Perhaps the following idea could be a reasonable path. If it really is going to be possible to have continued economic growth, we need to be certain that growth will be decoupled from consumption of non-renewable resources.

In the long run, growth can only be permitted to come from the renewable parts of the material system: living beings and fluid resources like water, wind and, above all, solar power.

The argument against eternal economic growth has been summed up in a pithy comment by the British naturalist and broadcaster Sir David Attenborough: 'Anyone who says we can have infinite growth in a finite environment is either a madman, or an economist.' He continued in a slightly more diplomatic tone, saying that economists will have to figure out the solution to the challenge, because he cannot. But he knows that humans have only *one infinite resource* available to us.

The Sun: the origin of all energy. Everything else is finite. So the answer to our questions is up there in the sky. That's physics.

If we just learn to harness solar energy to our advantage, it can work.

An empire where the sun never sets?

It's worth thinking about.

WHAT HAS THE APE LEARNED?

In which we fast-forward through history and economics – and possibly end up with some new insights.

CULTURE IS ALL THE THINGS WE HUMANS DO.
And cultures are in constant flux.

We adapt our lifestyle to the time and place we happen to live in. We simply do what we have to do to enjoy the best possible life wherever we happen to be. Nice and reasonable. But some things we do seem to remain largely unchanged. They are present in all ages and places. They recur. We can call it an axiom – a term borrowed from mathematics and philosophy, which denotes something so obvious that it requires no further investigation. It seems almost arrogant to claim that such a thing exists in a society, and that it requires no further investigation. But let's take a look. Our made-up ape and all her equally made-up descendants presumably encountered some conditions that became axiomatic at the very beginning of time. They were realisations about the world and existence that later accompanied us throughout human history. As we have seen, they would form the foundation of nearly every action we undertook.

One axiom is that not everything is present everywhere. For example, avocado trees do not grow everywhere. Neither do apricot trees. That's how the world has always been. It has been one of the conditions of our existence.

Another axiom is that most things are not present in infinite quantities. Quite the opposite. We may have thought some things were infinite, as we gazed out at an ocean or a vast glacier that stretched towards the horizon. Today, though, we know that all resources are finite. That's another thing we have had to accept. Both of these axioms were givens for our ape, way back then, just as they are for us and all her descendants.

Another axiom is that we humans are all different. We, and most other organisms, are not identical individuals. We have natural differences in our abilities.

Our ape quickly recognised these conditions in her life and adapted. Of course, we don't know exactly when and how we made specific adaptations. They are shrouded in the mists of time. But it was probably just by chance that apes discovered it was good to exchange things when not everyone had everything in the same amounts. Essentially the same story then as now, despite the long timeline – several million years, in fact. And a division of labour is good when not everyone can do everything. You gather nuts; I catch fish. And there you have it: now, we need each other. Cooperating is not just good, it can even be necessary when not everyone does everything or is able to. But, as we have seen, the best bit is that trading things means both parties end up better off. That made trading absolutely irresistible.

Trading became inseparable from us. Much of our long history consists of more of the same. We hunted, gathered and occasionally looked after one another in small nomadic groups. We exchanged some items once in a while. Sometimes, we fought too. There was no agriculture yet, no companies and no money – all those came much later. And this was undoubtedly the longest period in our history. No wonder we still retain some characteristics from that time. Our friends in evolutionary psychology like to point out that humans can be likened to a vast noisy herd of nouveau-riche nomads, who find it difficult to adapt to megacities, factories, smartphones and post-industrial lifestyles. Two hundred years of industry, preceded by around 10,000 years of simple agriculture, is barely the blink of an eye in evolutionary terms.

So our nature is probably the same in many respects, but our culture – what we do and don't do – has really changed. In our story, we have seen how we became settled and started to grow crops. Small villages began to spring up and then grew into cities – places for people eager to trade – bustling marketplaces, three millennia ago, in what is now called the Middle East, where we can find traces of the first hipster. You remember Kushim, the bookkeeper in the city of Uruk, who seemed interested in beer. We noted that our ape had really come a long way, even then. In cities, trading reached new heights and became what a modern economist would call *complex*. Complicated. We invented the art of writing and started noting things down to remember them. But, the more we traded, the more obvious it became that bartering has its shortcomings. While the city's marketplaces offered amazing new opportunities for trading, there were a number of niggling practical problems. Some goods were heavy or bulky, making them difficult to transport to the marketplace. Other goods had a short shelf life, such as fresh fish; people had to be found quickly to exchange them with. Some goods simply could not be stored. These recurring practical problems prompted us to take the next major step in our progress. We came up with a new item – money – which solved our problem by making trading easier.

But what actually is money? That was one of the ape's key questions. We have learned that money is a made-up item – it is based on an agreement that works as long as everyone believes in it. And, when everyone believes in money, we can use it to transform wine into fizzy water, and a sack of potatoes into a bottle of wine. We met a Swedish explorer and financial innovator by the name of Johan Palmstruch. He was living in 17th-century Amsterdam when he came up with the idea of starting a bank to lend money. After relocating to Stockholm, he launched his own bank, known as Stockholms Banco. He refined and streamlined *credit notes*, a banking product that was already popular. His brainwave was to issue *banknotes* in fixed denominations. Then someone with, say, a 100-kronor banknote could exchange banknotes with other people. Banknotes became a means of payment that could easily change owner: paper money. As it turned out, Palmstruch's bank went bust, but the Swedish state acquired it and made it into the Riksbank, which still exists today as Sweden's central bank – the oldest central bank in the world. It would be easy to believe that the king of Sweden took over the role of issuing money in the form of coins and notes. After all, the state had its own bank. But that's not what happened. It would take a few hundred years before the Swedish state started issuing money. In the meantime, banks in Sweden continued to issue their own money, right up until the early 20th century.

Of course, money and banks go together. But not always. Banks have always needed money. But, as we have learned in this narrative, money does not always need banks. Bitcoin and other cryptocurrencies need no bank. They are transferred directly from one user to another, just like any old email. And we have learned that anything can be money, as long as we agree. Before the advent of banknotes and coins, we experimented with everything from shells and salt to cattle and grain. There were no banks then, either. Borrowing and lending seed, corn and cattle had gone on for millennia before Christ. But nothing that was directly reminiscent of what we now know as banking. As we have seen, banks emerged quite late in our long history of trading – in Italy, in the 12th and 13th centuries.

There is a popular image of banks lending the money you and I have paid into our savings accounts. And then they collect a little interest. But that's not really how it works, the ape discovered. It's actually very far from the truth. Instead, banks practise a form of magic. Money is created out of nothing.

Ex nihilo. Abracadabra!

Nowadays, it's usually the result of someone borrowing money to buy a home. Let's take a look behind the scenes. You want to buy a house for €400,000. Unfortunately, you only have €80,000 in your savings account. You borrow the rest. First, the bank checks to make sure you appear to earn a good salary with a secure job and are not too risky a customer. You are deemed to be reliable. They have noted your income, subtracted your expenses and see that you appear to have some left over, enough to cover the loan, even if interest rates went up a bit. The house you want to buy is valued at €400,000. You get the loan. The bank credits itself with a new asset of €320,000. Your debt to the bank is the bank's asset. The bank will require monthly payments from you, with interest. And – *ka-ching* – 320,000 new euros are transferred to your account.

That's where the magic happened.

And it really did create new money. This is a job that keeps bank managers employed all over the world. The bank does need to have some money of its own, but only a few per cent – usually less than 10%. Most of their money the banks create themselves. So all the banks are printing their own money, figuratively speaking. In a way, we are back in the adventurer Johan Palmstruch's world, strangely enough – the man with Europe's first banknotes. Only around 3% of the money in Sweden today is in the form of banknotes and coins. The rest is digital – created by the banks.

The ape thinks: An e-krona would probably be a good idea. The Riksbank would repeat the same manoeuvre from the early 20th century, when the state assumed a monopoly on issuing banknotes and coins. Retail banks could no longer issue their own banknotes. That gave the Riksbank better control over the *monetary supply* – an important matter for a central bank.

In countries like Sweden, our bank branches have essentially stopped handling cash. Now, it's mostly ones and zeros flashing up on screen. But that flashing will have far greater effects on money and banking. We have seen how cypherpunks' dream of competing currencies is becoming a reality. Cryptocurrencies require no traditional banks or accounts. They zoom straight from the sender to the recipient. And the things a bank can and should do are also changing rapidly. We are far down inside the digital rabbit hole, now. As we know, some very curious things can happen there. Perhaps everyone in the world could even be able to transfer money to one another. As you will recall, around half the people in the world have no bank account.

The ape has also pondered that hand that – often, but not always – seems to make everything work in an economy. Adam Smith, the Scotsman often referred to as the first economist, came up with a famous metaphor about an invisible hand governing various markets. Millions of people's self-interest in maximising their benefit ensures that resources are utilised in the most efficient way possible. Bakers' bread generally ends up in the right place every morning. But we have also learned that the invisible hand needs a certain amount of guidance, funnily enough. It cannot solve everything on its own. Sometimes, it even causes problems. We have seen how markets and economies can crash. The hand also doesn't seem to care much about things like unfairness and high income inequality in society. The ape thinks about it. How much politics should there be in economics? And how much economics in politics? There are no clear answers.

The pendulum has swung back and forth, from the simple idea that the state and public authorities should involve themselves as little as possible, expressed as *laissez-faire* (meaning 'let them do' or 'let them go'), to the idea that the state should take on a major role, owning and controlling companies and markets. In the past four decades, since 1980, the pendulum has swung far in the first direction, towards letting the *market* decide. People have had great faith in market solutions, privatisation and deregulation. The pendulum got a strong push in that direction when the Berlin Wall fell in 1989 and when the Soviet Union collapsed a couple of years later. It seemed like confirmation that free markets were the answer to many questions, if perhaps not all. The American philosopher Francis Fukuyama even wrote a controversial book on the subject, entitled *The End of History and the Last Man*. Fukuyama said that, after the end of the Cold War and the fall of the Soviet Union, no alternative forms of human government remained. Nothing could compete with free-market liberal democracies, so the whole world should move in the same direction to become free-market liberal democracies.

Fukuyama's book had its critics from day one. Today, those critics have the wind in their sails. The pendulum has already returned from one extreme and is on its way in the opposite direction – again. Faith in the market's superiority took a big hit after the 2008 financial crisis – the second-largest economic crisis in modern times, after the 1929 stock-market crash. Europe, the USA and other countries attempted economic shock therapy by lowering interest rates to zero or negative figures, all to stimulate economic growth, to jump-start markets and make investments profitable, without the state having to pay too many pipers. Instead, governments should be frugal and pay off their debts. The stimulus was intended for the market, which was supposed to do the job. It ended up being a lengthy course of shock therapy that lasted more than ten years.

And the markets kept going – until tiny uninvited guests put a stop to the whole global trading party in the spring of 2020: the novel coronavirus. Huge government support packages were rolled out during and after the pandemic, all over the world. Each country had its own particular version. But they all had the same aim. Mass extinction of businesses, unemployment and (in the longer term) depression had to be avoided at all costs, and fast. Of course, cutting interest rates already at or below zero would produce little in the way of results. Besides, interest-rate cuts are relatively slow-acting. That's where the pendulum swung back. Letting things run their course was no longer an option.

So, various forms of government support helped the global economy weather the effects of entire cities and regions shutting down, avoiding major disasters. But the aggressive little coronavirus, combined with Russia's invasion of Ukraine, has reminded us just how vulnerable a globally intertwined economy is to disruptions. Production shutdowns have driven up prices for food and energy. An old acquaintance from the past made an unexpected return to the economic scene: namely, inflation. Soon, we might have customs barriers again. The big party, sometimes called *globalisation*, where countries and regions all contribute the things they're good at, requires an open world. The more open, the better. It's the opposite of a world in which societies and countries shut down and cut themselves off to shield themselves against aggressive people or microbes. Once the gunpowder smoke has settled and the virus fog has dispersed, the route back to the big global village will presumably be a long one. Maybe, the ape thinks, it was just an aberration.

But our eternal trading will continue in one form or another. We will find new routes. As we have learned in our story here, the benefits of large markets and trade zones are very appealing. There are more people to do business with. There are opportunities for large-scale operations and specialisation. And everyone can contribute with their particular strengths. A sort of economic bring-your-own party. All the benefits of the international bring-your-own party helped the process of globalisation to lift several billion people out of poverty in just three or four decades. It's unlikely we will abandon it entirely. But, in the shadow of missiles, viruses and CO_2, we can probably expect our marketplaces to change in some ways. For example, we can count on trading with our nearby allies to be big for the foreseeable future. In times of increasing uncertainty, we often prefer 'home sweet home' and like-minded people.

But, as we have seen, history rarely comes to an end. The benefits of large markets are another axiom that prompts us to build ever bigger cities and venture out into the world. Despite our current crises and unease, we still live in a world where skills, possessions and resources are not evenly distributed among people or places around the world. Avocado trees still don't grow in Scandinavia. We need to trade. We will try to open up the world again, building trade and exchange with partners around the globe. Maybe it will happen with new technology, maybe in different areas than before. Maybe it will take decades. But we will come back. You can rely on axioms – they're always there in the background, making things happen.

We try to build our lives as best we can under the prevailing circumstances. It's always about the self-interest, the ape thinks. Self-interest is also there in the background and is – you guessed it – another axiom. We have seen how the vast complex mechanism we call the global economy is fundamentally driven by billions of people's self-interest in living as well as they can. And the sum total of all these people's individual interests and efforts – without any overall boss – are transformed into something in everyone's interest. Back in the 18th century, Adam Smith, the man with the invisible hand, was fascinated by the way a baker was motivated by self-interest, rather than love for all mankind, to get up early and bake.

Millions upon millions of self-interests competing with one another – that's one way to view an economy. Even the global economy. And it's understandable why we're always coming up with new things. Sometimes, it can even seem ridiculous, with all the new things we come up with. But it's no wonder, now that we know that everyone's self-interest is competing with everyone else's. You've got to find your own thing, the place where you can become the best baker, the best singer, or whatever you're interested in. Sometimes, a company or product can achieve something like a monopoly. It's simply found a niche in the miraculous economic mechanism of competing self-interests where it is apparently unthreatened – for a while, anyway. We can find examples in every sector. For a while, the Swedish car manufacturer Volvo had a virtual monopoly if you wanted to buy a safe car. Today, a number of online 'platform companies' – such as Facebook, Google and Alibaba – are in a similar position. An Austrian economist named Joseph Schumpeter called this phenomenon a *temporary monopoly*. Every entrepreneur's dream is to find the sweet spot, a moment in time when their product is perceived as unique. Everyone wants or needs it – for a while. Usually, a monopoly is temporary. We have seen how Apple's iPhone knocked out a whole industry of traditional mobile-phone manufacturers.

The mechanism of the economy, with all its self-interests, is like the god Shiva, the ape thinks. Shiva is the Hindu god of creation and destruction. All new creation has its evil twin in destruction. The new displaces the old.

But success and happiness at the individual level do not always equate to undiluted joy at societal level. Companies that gain a dominant position grow sluggish over time. Why make an effort when you're already number one? It usually leads to inefficiency, abuse of power and dissatisfied customers in the long run. That's why pure monopolies are prohibited in most countries. Monopolies also limit freedom of choice – not good. The ape wants to have a choice. Opposition to monopolies is just one small example of how choice can be encouraged. Not having central planning seems to work too. Various large and small-scale attempts at alternatives to a free-market economy and the invisible hand have been made in the past 150 years. Various centrally planned systems in which the invisible hand was replaced with the highly visible hands of tens of thousands of bureaucrats have been tried in a number of countries. The biggest, most spectacular attempt was made in the Soviet Union, a centrally planned communist state, where five-year plans replaced the free choices of buyers and sellers. After long-term stagnation, desperate shortages and attempts at reforms to get the planned system to work more efficiently, the Soviet Union collapsed in 1991. It took most of the world's other planned economies down with it. The invisible hand took over most of the world's nations over the next three decades. In the early 2020s, just one country continued to hold on to the idea of a visible, centrally planned hand, despite great hardship: namely, North Korea.

Over time, the ape learned that all resources are finite, and the Sun is the source of all energy. We couldn't have known that at the dawn of time. There were so few of us and the world was so, so big. We knew so little, back then. Now, we know. It's been established through research. There is no such thing as a *weightless* economy. The economy's magic trick, where wheat is transformed into wine, or a taxi ride is exchanged for money, can sometimes seem weightless – to say nothing of the financial economy or the video-game industry, where we buy, sell and use purely made-up items that exist only in the virtual world. But, if we stop to think about it, we need a screen, a cable, a sender or receiver. Technology and software always have a material basis, some sort of hardware. And, in the service economy, we always need some*one* – a fellow human – or some*thing* – a machine – to perform a service. Economic processes are always chemical, biological and physical somewhere along the way. Your weightless bitcoins suddenly land – *plop* – in the construction of a half-mile-long server centre in a forest near you. It always starts in nature and always ends there. That's another axiom. Even bitcoin and all its illustrious successors down the rabbit hole have to obey that principle.

Even the word *economics* refers to the idea of getting by on scarce resources. Budgeting. *Oikos* is Greek for 'household' and *nomos* means 'law.' What resources do we have to budget, at the end of the day? How big is our budget? As we saw in chapter six, about the Earth, we have to conclude that our budget and the Earth are one and the same. Our planet is the outer limit of the economy. It includes everything in the budget. Today, we also know that we have nothing that is *outside* the system, *outside* the economy. That's what the ape thinks. That's a major departure from how the classical – and particularly the neoclassical – economist chaps with their bushy whiskers viewed matters, and from the mainstream view for much of the 20th century. They regarded the economy as more of a man-made system, independent of nature – a bit like the way we regarded ourselves as a species: not really as animals among other animals. Sometimes, economics produced unintended side effects outside the economic sphere. These came to be called *externalities* and concerned phenomena beyond the intended result of economic trans-actions between two parties, which affected a third party. An external effect can be positive or negative, but we usually talk about negative externalities, such as a body of water that is devastated when a nearby factory expels warm water used for cooling. Really, though, instead of *externalities*, we should be calling them *internalities*. They are right here in our big round household – the Earth.

Everything needs to have a price attached to it. Air, water and all the other natural resources around us. Everything needs to be included in the economy. The outer limit of the economy's capacity is set by the Earth's limits. There are certain critical levels that mark the limit of what the Earth can tolerate in terms of pollution – if we're going to live here, at any rate. Those levels form a definite physical framework for all economic activity. This is also an axiom. Our economic system can develop within this framework. The American economist Herman Daly created a simple diagram to show how our prosperity comes from two sources. The economy is a little square in the middle of a large circle, which represents the ecosystem. From the economy, the economic system, we get human-created capital, and from nature, we get natural capital. Both give us well-being. If well-being – which is derived from the economy – increases sufficiently, the square starts to take up a larger proportion of the circle. Eventually, the corners of the square touch the perimeter of the circle. The Earth starts to get full, and the space for nature shrinks. Then, the share of our well-being derived from nature also shrinks. The ape thinks it's a nice, visual way of illustrating the equilibrium.

The only thing that enters the system from outside, as an input to the Earth and the economy, is solar energy – that's what kicks everything off and makes things keep going. There is a clear, well-researched link between energy consumption and economic growth. Our economy is dependent on added energy, in one form or another. Or still another form. Usually, in every possible form at once. Some energy, such as fossil fuels, can take a detour down into the Earth's sedimentary layers for a few million years. Fossil fuels come from plants that converted solar energy into carbon via photosynthesis – and then were subject to pressure under the Earth's surface for a very, very long time, until they became coal, oil and natural gas. We extracted these from the ground and used them to fire up the Industrial Revolution. As we have seen, the resulting pace was unprecedented.

We used coal to power steam engines; steam locomotives could chug along the railways.

We used coal to make steel, with which we built bridges and factories.

We used oil to make petrol and aviation fuel.

We used steel and glass to build skyscrapers.

But basic energy sources in today's high-tech economy come from nature. Yes, indeed. So, if we are going to have a system that functions properly in the long term, nature has to be treated as an *internality*, not an *externality*.

Last but definitely not least: the ape has learned about happiness. What does the economy produce? What about our economic system? The ape thinks that the economy is fundamentally people who want to create happiness – joy in the everyday, a nicer life for everyone involved. Many routes lead to that goal – and people are always finding new ones. Viewed through a physical lens, the economy produces loads of things in the form of products, buildings and infrastructure. Tasty meals, air conditioning, sneakers, hair conditioner and medicines. Electric vehicles, streaming services and doggy treats. An absolutely vast rainforest of goods and services that make us happier and more satisfied with life – for a while, anyway. Along with a lot of junk – all the waste and pollution and packaging that's left after all the production and consumption. Some of it is generated in the production stage; some is garbage left after we have consumed the item. It goes back into the environment. Even a house that stands for centuries is gradually broken down. Some bits crumble away. They can be replaced with new parts, but eventually the new parts also crumble. All of this is a physical, biological process. But it's only the means, not the end. What we are really trying to create is a good feeling. Prosperity. Well-being.

Economics in its modern form emerged in the 18th century as a moral philosophy. As we have seen, it concerns something far more existential than the mere exchange of things. It goes beyond numbers. Instead, it concerns a philosophy of happiness and the path to happiness. Ultimately, economics is about how we can try to make life a little better – for each individual or for society as a whole – and how we can get more from the resources – the budget – we have, to make optimum use of them.

The better we get at cooperating, the more well-being we will create together. For centuries, the economy has had a bit of a bad reputation because profit has been associated with greed and selfishness. Economists have been bad at explaining what we call *win-win solutions*: both parties ending up better off from a deal. That element that was there at the dawn of time, when two hominids traded figs for nuts. Both ended up better off. That's the core of cooperation and the free-market economy. It's the source of added value, in the form of money and/or increased happiness when two parties exchange items.

In chapter four, about the magical mechanism, we learned some of the finer philosophical points about what economics really is. Ever since the 18th century, economic theorists like Adam Smith have done the world a disservice by using the term *self-interest*. Most of us instinctively regard self-interest as something negative. But what Smith wanted to show was how the sum of many people's self-interest adds up to something good for everyone – good for the *common interest*. You may remember the important detail that *self-interest* is not the opposite of *kindness*. Self-interest is not the same as *meanness*. Self-interest, in the sense described by Adam Smith, always contains an element of mutuality. In the example with the baker, he doesn't operate his bakery out of kindness. He doesn't give his bread away. Instead, the baker is motivated by serving the *common interest* between himself and his customers. He needs to bake tasty, reasonably priced bread. The baker needs customers. Customers need the baker. If they are to make a deal, it has to be a *win-win solution*.

Self-interest, profit – economics can be described in those terms.

Common interests, cooperation, added happiness – economics can also be described in those terms.

Growth is the means, not the end. That's one of the most important messages in this book. The aim of economics – exchanging goods for services, or services for other services – is better quality of life. Happiness. Health. A better life.

Even our society and our economy are based on those ideas. The entire Western world is based on the notion that economic growth leads to better health, more happiness, comfort. But growth is merely a simplified metric for measuring those things.

For many decades, we have measured economic activity in society in terms of GDP, which stands for Gross Domestic Product. We do this because increasing GDP used to work well as a rough measure of increased well-being. *More* was equivalent to *good*.

As we saw in chapter seven, on happiness, there are many reasons to criticise the used of economic growth as a measure of happiness. And there are many possible alternatives, other metrics, that might better reflect what we *really* want to achieve: prosperity, well-being.

We can discuss how that metric should look, which tools are best.

That task lies before us.

We'll need to help each other to keep the goal in sight.

A better existence.

A good life.

Happiness.

Smile.

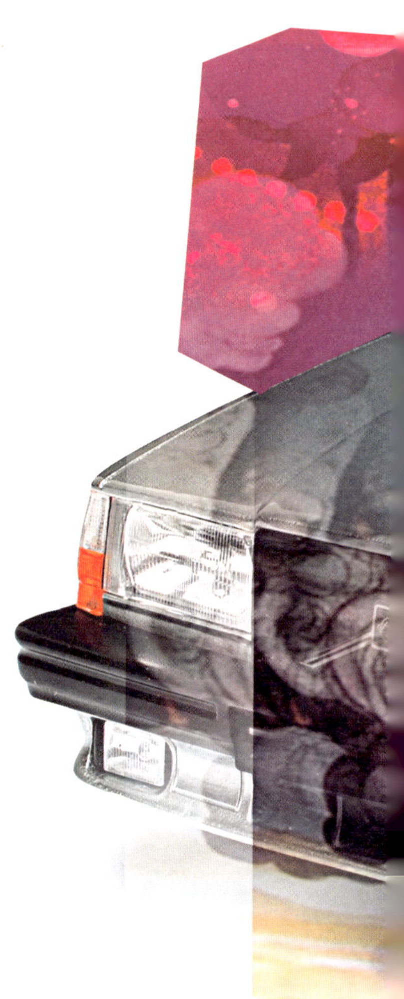

Want to find out more?
Bibliography and further reading

Daly, Herman E., *From Uneconomic Growth to a Steady-State Economy* (Cheltenham: Edward Elgar Publishing, 2014).

Fukuyama, Francis, *The End of History and the Last Man* (London: Penguin Books, 1992).

Harari, Yuval Noah, *Sapiens – A Brief History of Humankind* (London: Random House, 2015).

Kirkland, Stephane, *Paris Reborn: Napoléon III, Baron Haussmann and the Quest to Build a Modern City* (New York: Picador, 2014).

McCloskey, Deirdre N., *Bourgeois Equality: How Ideas, Not Capital or Institutions, Enriched the World* (Chicago: University of Chicago Press, 2016).

May, Timothy C., *The Crypto Anarchist Manifesto* (1988) https://groups.csail.mit.edu/mac/classes/6.805/articles/crypto/cypher-punks/may-crypto-manifesto.html (accessed 21 September 2022).

Montgomery, David R., *Dirt: The Erosion of Civilizations* (Berkeley: University of California Press, 2007).

Nakamoto, Satoshi, *Bitcoin: A Peer-to-Peer Electronic Cash System* (2008) https://nakamotoinstitute.org/bitcoin/ (accessed 21 September 2022).

Piketty, Thomas, *Capital in the Twenty-First Century*, tr. Arthur Goldhammer (Cambridge: Harvard University Press, 2017).

Raworth, Kate, *Doughnut Economics: Seven Ways to Think Like a 21st-Century Economist* (London: Random House, 2017).

Shorto, Russell, *Amsterdam: A History of the World's Most Liberal City* (New York: Vintage Books, 2014).

Smith, Adam, *The Wealth of Nations, Books I–III* (London: Penguin Classics, 1982).

Engine for table of differences
IBM

THE MONKEY AND THE MONEY
A history of capitalism

PUBLISHED BY BOKFÖRLAGET STOLPE, STOCKHOLM, SWEDEN, 2023

© THE AUTHOR AND BOKFÖRLAGET STOLPE 2023

ORIGINAL TITLE: *Apan och kapitalet – en ekonomisk historia*

TEXT: KJELL A. NORDSTRÖM

TRANSLATION: RUTH URBOM

EDITOR: JAN RYDÉN BONMOT

TEXT EDITOR: PENELOPE PRICE

ILLUSTRATIONS: PATRIK INSTEDT AND
ANNE GUSTAFSSON (PAGE 4, 174 AND 191)

DESIGN: NINA ULMAJA

LAYOUT: PONTUS DAHLSTRÖM

PREPRESS AND PRINT COORDINATOR: ITALGRAF MEDIA AB, SWEDEN

PRINT: PRINTON, ESTONIA, VIA ITALGRAF MEDIA, 2023

FIRST EDITION, FIRST PRINTING

ISBN: 978-91-89425-71-2

BOKFÖRLAGET STOLPE IS A PART OF
AXEL AND MARGARET AX:SON JOHNSON
FOUNDATION FOR PUBLIC BENEFIT

BOKFÖRLAGET STOLPE

AXEL AND MARGARET AX:SON JOHNSON
FOUNDATION FOR PUBLIC BENEFIT